"*Refreshed!* If I were asked to use one
for a Deeper Faith, it would be, 'Refreshed!' Each page is like taking a deep
breath of fresh, crisp, clean mountain air. While it may be tempting to read
multiple sections per day, I encourage you to read only one and let it resonate
throughout the day. Each 'shift' offers a wealth of insight that can occupy
your thought life for one full rotation of the earth."

Reverend Mark Fitter, founder of Pastors in Transition

"There's something about Dean Del Sesto's perspective that speaks to
me more powerfully than most other authors, especially on this topic of
strengthening our relationship with God and others. I think it's because
Dean is a business leader—he processes his own relationship with God and
others through a pragmatic lens. As a result, his challenges and epiphanies
are quite bold, intentional, direct, and convicting. This is a book you'll
read if you're ready to have someone do some deep work with your soul
(in a good way)."

Shelley Leith, director of church relations,
Zondervan; coauthor, *Character Makeover*

"As you read this book, it will read you. By combining powerful biblical
exhortations with quick, convicting points of application, Dean provides a
clear mirror to help Christians see themselves more honestly. Dean's goal:
honest spiritual evaluations followed by realistic applications for a deeper
walk with the living God. Goal achieved!"

Chaplain R. Steve Lowe, founder and president,
Pacific Youth Correctional Ministries

"Dean Del Sesto writes with such precision and insight that it illumines the
deep spiritual truths that otherwise can get lost in their complexity. This book
is enlightening, vision casting, and immensely accessible to anyone desiring
to experience more of God in their everyday lives."

Jeff Tacklind, pastor; author,
The Winding Path of Transformation

"Beware! Dean Del Sesto's latest book may well 'afflict the comfortable and
comfort the afflicted!' For those on the Christian path who desire a deeper
experience of God and his promised abundant life, Dean offers insightful
wisdom and concrete challenges to help us clean out the cobwebs of limiting beliefs and behaviors. With flashes of brilliance, he points out our habits
of falling into lethargic and mechanical prayer, service, and relationships
with God and others. But he doesn't leave us without vision for a different
way! Offering a recommended question to ponder or practice to embrace, he
helps us move down the road toward change and deeper growth. *Shift Your*

Thinking for a Deeper Faith offers insights and challenges that will energize your personal devotional life and serve as a rich source of discussion with friends and groups."

Helen Steinkamp, cofounder, Marketplace Women;
retreat facilitator; spiritual director

"Dean Del Sesto's writing is more than good; it's extraordinarily thought provoking. Here's one of his witticisms that catches the reader as Dean encourages us to consider how we relate to others on a daily basis with our eyes: 'Eye contact = I contact.' Most devotional-style books are limited by how much can be said in a one-page format. Dean is a master of one-liners and deep, sophisticated thinking. He takes just one page to share fresh ideas, new perspectives, inspiration, and motivation designed to help us contemplate and apply spiritual truths in a unique and fresh way."

Milan Yerkovich, founder, Relationship 180;
marriage counselor; coauthor, *How We Love* and
How We Love Our Kids; cohost of the nationally
syndicated counseling talk show *New Life Live!*

"For most people, time multiplies their words but clouds their perspectives. Classrooms often add syllables while they subtract clarity. Most of us long for someone who can take the most challenging subject and reduce it to wisdom that can be understood and then incorporated. In this book, Dean addresses the most foundational questions of the Christian life and illuminates them in ways that will allow the thoughtful reader to come to new convictions that are, upon engagement, transformational. Take the time to ponder these pages; you'll never be the same."

Bob Shank, CEO, The Master's Program;
author, *LifeMastery*

"I really love this book and I need this book even more. Too often I find short-format Christian writing to be pithy, though the truths in *Shift Your Thinking for a Deeper Faith* cut deep and beg for a response. I am grateful this book exists for followers of Jesus like myself as it challenges the cruise-control habits of our faith and compassionately presents a more fulfilling way to follow after the heart of God. Dean is a master wordsmith and truth-teller, and we get the opportunity to listen in."

Ryan Leith, psychotherapist

"There are times when coming up with topics to discuss at small groups or meetings can be a challenge. *Shift Your Thinking for a Deeper Faith* has 99 of them that will spur great conversations and resonate at a deep level with how we can be living out our Christian life. It firmly but gracefully connects the reader to what God says is true, inspiring us to live a fuller life simply by abiding in what is inherently ours."

"Dean's brilliance is in his ability to give words that readers crave in their soul but don't always know how to say. If you're needing a fresh take on your way forward, you've just found it."

"It's refreshing when a book comes along that offers so many transformational perspectives to bring more fulfillment to our Christian life and our relationship with God and others. Powerful yet graceful, Dean encourages new thinking to help us live to our potential—spiritually, personally, and professionally."

"*Shift Your Thinking for a Deeper Faith* offers insights into how to live your faith differently and look through the lens of how you may serve others and the kingdom in richer ways. His books are disrupters—as he says, dismantling comes before reassembly can begin. Read it and reap!"

"Dean's thoughtful humility and penetrating insights call us into a deeper consideration of what it means to lead a sustainably meaningful life of faith. I am grateful for the invitation to examine who or what I have put my faith in from moment to moment throughout my day."

"There are a lot of books that invite you to a richer way of living the Christian life; to have more of what God has to offer us. This book does it in a way that is intensely practical and is rare in its direct approach. It is also unique in that it covers so many aspects of our walk. It's like a lot of books in one. If you're looking to live a more confident, clear life, one in which your relationship with God and others moves to a new level of intimacy and fulfillment, read this book!"

"This book gracefully disrupts the beliefs and assumptions about what doesn't work on a Christian's journey through life and is chock-full of straight-to-the-point wisdom. If you reflect upon and attempt to apply what you read, I believe you will experience more of what Jesus calls 'the abundant life': one full of more joy and peace even in the midst of chaos and significant challenges. It may well disrupt some of your long-standing spiritual perspectives, and if so, they may be replaced with those truths that our Lord truly wants us all to experience."

Dr. Darrell Passwater, former professor, Crowell School
of Business, Biola University; Convene chair

"Dean Del Sesto has clearly been called to step into our busy lives as hardworking Christians with the ongoing reminder to keep God in the center of all aspects of life, business, and relationships. It's in times like we're in today when we need bold, active Christians to live out their faith, positively influencing and inspiring those who are lost and bringing God into the equation. Dean's most recent book, *Shift Your Thinking for a Deeper Faith*, is an excellent read based on biblical truths that will challenge, inspire, and encourage you to live in the fullness of what God has for you and others."

Paul Aubin, VP on the executive leadership team of Convene;
elder at Mariners Church in Irvine, CA;
author of adoption-focused books

SHIFT YOUR THINKING
FOR A
DEEPER FAITH

Books by Dean Del Sesto

Shift Your Thinking
A Shift a Day for Your Best Year Yet
Shift Your Thinking for Success
Shift Your Thinking for a Deeper Faith

SHIFT YOUR THINKING

FOR A
DEEPER FAITH

99 WAYS TO STRENGTHEN
YOUR RELATIONSHIP WITH GOD,
OTHERS, AND YOURSELF

DEAN DEL SESTO

Revell

a division of Baker Publishing Group
Grand Rapids, Michigan

Published by Revell
a division of Baker Publishing Group
PO Box 6287, Grand Rapids, MI 49516-6287
www.revellbooks.com

Printed in the United States of America

Library of Congress Cataloging-in-Publication Control Number: 2019007001

978-0-8007-2899-1

In keeping with biblical principles of creation stewardship, Baker Publishing Group advocates the responsible use of our natural resources. As a member of the Green Press Initiative, our company uses recycled paper when possible. The text paper of this book is composed in part of post-consumer waste.

19 20 21 22 23 24 25   7 6 5 4 3 2 1

There are so many people to thank who had a profound impact on my writing this book. Their commitment to the Lord, wisdom, and insights I've learned over the years have allowed me to see in practice how all God's words, when embraced, create an amazing new life from the moment of belief. I am grateful most of all to my wife, Kitt, who has shown me God's love in practice and has inspired my heart, thinking, and the desire to be a better husband, man, and friend. And Lord, you are the author and finisher of my faith and I am eternally grateful.

It's **ironic** that we

trust God

for our **eternity**

but often **question**

whether he'll handle the

day-to-day issues

we contend with in our life.

Introduction

> The quickest, most transformative growth in our Christian walk will come from the real-time acceptance of what God has *already* promised us. The depth of that acceptance will be directly proportional to the victory we will live in.

Ask any Bible-believing Christian if they would like to have a more rewarding, intimate relationship with God and others—as well as more confidence, wisdom, and influence—and I'm certain the answer would be a resounding yes. But often the mechanics of the process become lost in the shuffle of a busy life. We lose sight of what God has said is true about our infinite value, gifts, and extraordinary strength: *you know* . . . those things that were installed in us at salvation but are often forgotten or shelved as we live out our life. Add to that the recycled, inconsistent, or mechanical ways we can engage with our basic spiritual disciplines, and our spiritual growth and life progress end up moving at the speed of rust.

> For in Christ all the fullness of the Deity lives in bodily form, and in Christ you have been brought to fullness. He is the head over every power and authority.
>
> Colossians 2:9–10

Some Hard Truths . . .

It's not hard to see and experience that many believers are living their lives partially embracing the hundreds of promises God gave us about the abundance of spiritual assets we have in him. This disconnectedness shows up in things like the weights and burdens we attach to adversity and basic conflicts; lifestyle agitation and difficulty; the trepidation or fear we experience with opportunity, promotion, and adventure; and the fatigue, mood swings, and defeat we can feel simply doing everyday life. We end up in a cycle of intermittent faith: a life that is controlled more by external events than internal resolve and where the fruit of the Spirit is more contingent on how we feel in the moment than on what is actually true about our identity in Christ. Because the Spirit of God is within us, the practice of living from the inside out rather than the "outside in" creates a new beginning of moving away from reactionary, unstable, and stress-infused beliefs and actions to more insightful, peaceful, and positive responses to everything that happens in our life, *good or bad!*

Don't just long for God's kingdom to be revealed in the future. Discover it in present moments.

The good news is that experiencing the fullness of God is a simple equation; it's not always easy, but the mechanics are simple.

It requires that we *intentionally* stay connected to what God has shared in his Word about what is true; by connected, I mean we weld and temper the truths of God's promises (his Word) onto every aspect of our attitude, mindset, emotions, and actions—not just on occasions when we happen to land on a spiritual high but in the moments of every day. The quality and consistency of this connection (this welding) determines everything that we do and how we process all that happens. The questions become clear: Will I live my life based on what *I or others invent as real* or what *God has said is true*? And if I don't know or have not committed these truths to memory, will I get schooled up in these promises so I can access them at a moment's notice?

> I have told you these things, so that in me you may have peace. In this world you will have trouble. But take heart! I have overcome the world.
>
> John 16:33

If I had to put a percentage to it, I'd assert that most of the value and effectiveness of our day-to-day Christian walk comes from our capacity to respond to all of life through the lens of God's promises. This practice has a way of taking a mindset filled with too many question marks and replacing them with more confident exclamation points, making life more consistent and fulfilling. From owning the amazing work he said is *already complete* in each of us to the arsenal of weaponry we have to our eternal security, we thrive by allowing the rhythm of those blessings to drive all we are and everything we do. We consciously choose that easy yoke and light burden we often hear about but seldom experience.

For our benefit (or better yet, *use*), God provided hundreds of promises, (aka—life guarantees) to make a powerful yet seemingly elusive point: we have been equipped with everything we need to live in victory, serve others, and have dominion over everything here on earth—every thought, emotion, relationship, agenda, problem, vision . . . you name it! This means that as a believer, the only thing we need to move toward in this life is a more resolute acceptance and ownership of what is already done in us—then live freely and confidently in recognition of that while loving God and loving others. The full power of God's resources is never an attainment or an achievement away, it is always a *belief* away: trusting what God said is true about the brilliant nature of you and all you *currently* possess!

Take these four truths, for example. Just these few realities alone will transform your life if you understand what is already complete in you and not some level you have yet to achieve or acquire.

1. You *already have* unlimited power and wisdom available in God.
2. He delivers value in *all* your present circumstances, catastrophic or not.
3. His Spirit resides inside you and can never leave you, *ever*, so you currently carry his presence and power.
4. All the fruit of the Spirit is available at full potency through aligning our thoughts to God's Word and renewing our mind.

There are many more truths to learn, but the practice and eventual habit of embracing our inheritance through just these four promises before any conversation, meeting, initiative, or vision will bring our spiritual assets to an on-demand status. As for the outcomes of this real-time adoption, they will be nothing short of, *well again* . . . what he has already promised! There are hundreds of these promises, and we will uncover many in this book along with other key empowering truths to improve your life every day.

Shift Your Thinking for a Deeper Faith (SYTFDF) is a book that will challenge you on how you live your life in relationship to the diversity and depth of God's promises. I know, because while writing it, it challenged and convicted me in every area of my life and helped me get honest about my walk with the Lord: whose voice(s) I listen to and what I believe in, *and don't*. SYTFDF was written to be a series of graceful yet forthright interruptions to the thinking and behavior that doesn't align with what God said is true about himself, you, and your journey as a believer. Not every point will be relevant to you, as you may be thriving in various areas of your life. For these points, consider the nuances that may serve you and move on. Perhaps other points will touch on a behavior or belief you hold and move you to think differently with an open mind and heart.

Getting the Most from This Book

This book is not a series of instructions on how to live your Christian life based on my experiences, knowledge, or background. Even though I live a blessed life, I'll spare you the agony of a "mimic me" approach; I have enough life experience to know that telling you what to do wouldn't serve you well, as we are all different. It is, however, a book based on God's Word that will cast a bright light on things rarely talked about; as mentioned, it will confront any ways-of-being or beliefs that don't work in life and ask you to consider new ways and beliefs that might.

A word of caution: it is in the *honest acceptance and awareness of what doesn't work in our lives* that the process of healing and change can begin. In other words, what you read in this book will likely do some dismantling in certain areas before reassembly can begin. I'll admit, the process of dismantling is a short-term discomfort, but it is nothing compared to the long-term discomfort of living a life with behaviors and beliefs that limit our potential to live as God intended. There is always more for us to access in God's kingdom, and it is often only a shift in thinking needed to bring greater fulfillment into our lives.

The goal of SYTFDF, however, isn't *just* about helping you get more during your journey as a believer in Christ, although I believe in my heart that will happen. The core principles on each page lean toward helping you *serve more* into others' lives while on your faith journey. This book is about deepening your faith in God and accessing the fullness of his provisions so you can shine brightly on others and, in turn, strengthen all aspects of your Christian walk.

Read at a Pace Instead of a Race

While reading SYTFDF, note there is not necessarily an advantage to reading the book sequentially, as there is no planned connection between the points. Although they all work together for our growth, they also stand on their own, meaning you could read from the end of the book backward or start in the middle and poke around and still experience the same impact. As for the pace, my strong recommendation is to read one or two points a day or a week, as the goal is not to move through the points in rhythm as if reading a novel: the goal is to integrate the relevant points you read into your life, career, and relationships so transformation becomes obvious, joyful, and sustainable. I ask that you read until you come to a place where you can bring what touches you into your life—the laboratory where real things happen, can be measured, and are improved.

We'll cover many areas of our Christian walk and may hit certain topics from a couple different angles. Regardless of your approach, my prayer is that your investment of time spent within these pages helps you grow closer to God and others in fresh, new ways. It is also my prayer that this book helps you love yourself in light of who God says you are while further aligning every aspect of you and your life to God's many sovereign realities.

1. Maintaining Balance in Life

> A fulfilled life is one where all areas
> are growing while no one area spikes
> at the expense of the others.

But seek first his kingdom and his righteousness, and all
these things will be given to you as well.

Matthew 6:33

There are many areas in our life that need our attention. Each area
is a living entity that requires an infusion of care daily, otherwise the
area suffers slowly until we start breathing life into it once again.
Although it may seem impossible to have all areas of our life growing congruently—areas such as spiritual life, work, spouse, kids,
health, friendships, ministry, hobbies, social activities, and fun—it
is possible and frankly necessary for a fulfilled and balanced life.

Caring for the various aspects of our life in a
healthy state is a balancing act—a noble one.

The foundation of having balance in life is always a healthy relationship with God. If that relationship is anemic in any way, it's a no-brainer that every other area of our life will not function in its full capacity. In the balance game, any one area of our life going sideways can make most days miserable. For example, if we don't care for our health, we will live in a moody, mentally foggy state, lacking the energy and focus needed to accomplish what God puts on our heart. Or consider the effects of a relationship that is suffering, where both parties are discontent, perhaps just existing and dealing with life as opposed to winning in life. This kind of relational breakdown can cast a dark shadow over everything and everyone connected to it because life will be looked at through the lens of pain and hopelessness. Then there's our careers, and the financial and emotional burdens that can occur if things are not cared for there. Life naturally cross-pollinates, all individual areas affecting the holistic reality of our experience.

One would think that life balance is something that takes discipline, and it does. But more than discipline, it takes faith knowing that God will honor our attention to balance. It is supported by his instruction throughout his Word to be a steward over *all* of areas of life in ways that glorify him and are an example to others. God knows that some areas of life can easily become idols, where our overattention or addiction to them can leave other areas ignored, causing a breakdown in those areas.

It's best to see our life as rooted in a close relationship with our Lord. And it's wise to accept that one or two areas thriving while others suffer brings nowhere near the fulfillment or future as when all areas are growing. And even though all areas may grow a little slower, the "all areas growing" commitment will leave little room for the enemy to gain entry to use any area of breakdown to taint the rest of life. *Give all areas of your life the attention they deserve today.*

The Question: Is my life in balance or are there areas that are in need of attention that will be in jeopardy if I don't make a commitment to strengthen them?

2. Prayer without Distraction

Engage in prayer with focus, humility,
and unwavering intentionality.

Very early in the morning, while it was still dark, Jesus got up,
left the house and went off to a solitary place, where he prayed.

Mark 1:35

The way we enter into a quick prayer or dedicated prayer time
is one of those overlooked topics that rarely finds its way onto
the pulpit or into text. Prayer has become an assumed practice
for most, but the components of prayer and the difference it can
make (whether praying for a meal or for healing from cancer) are
rarely examined. And yet, prayer is one of the foundational tenets
of our faith development. Prayer has serious impact on our relationship with God and others, so it demands a close inspection
from time to time.

Not every prayer is answered, but undistracted talking
and listening to God is always an answer to prayer.

Many times, the place in which we pray is riddled with actual or potential distractions and the casual, unfocused, unintentional way we stumble into prayer will have us distracted before we get started. Sometimes we'll close our eyes without giving much thought to what we'll pray for; we just open our mouths and before our heart has a chance to catch up to our words, the basic obligation of prayer time is over. It becomes a matter of checking the prayer box, when checking our hearts might serve us better.

The biggest impediment to a rewarding and effective prayer life is to engage with a mind that is so unfocused or distracted that *our presence* and *God's presence* elude us, making the process mostly mechanical instead of relational and spiritual.

More than anything, God wants *the pure, present* us in prayer time with no façades, judgments, idols, or baggage, and "going through the motions" approaches are banned for good. He wants us raw, ready to dialogue and receive his fullness without the deterrents of self in an environment where we can hear only him and not our internal chatter or external noise.

He wants us to talk, yes, but he is always speaking so he wants us to listen in direct relation to our specific prayers. Consider this: if God knows what we are praying for before we ask, what is he looking for when we pray? Perhaps it's the posture of our hearts, a commitment to faith, a grateful disposition, and a spirit of humility. When we pray like this, we receive enough spirit to conquer the day, instead of the day conquering us. *Consider bringing your prayer life to a new level of focus and intentionality today.*

The Question: What baggage or distractions do I bring to prayer time that no longer have a place?

3. Releasing the Bondage of Sin

> Your sin was *nailed* to the cross . . .
> so stop *hammering yourself*!

It is for freedom that Christ has set us free. Stand firm, then, and do not let yourselves be burdened again by a yoke of slavery.

Galatians 5:1

Consider the sin in your life, no matter how small or big you think it may be. Perhaps there's gluttony, doubt, pornography use, lying, pride, or other sins that are alive and well or looming in the corridors of your heart. Some sins may be chronic, others may show up on occasion when we feel like we need to medicate ourselves with sin to alleviate certain pains inherent to life.

Regardless of what brand of sin you are using to satisfy yourself or ease the difficulties of life and make it more bearable, a major breakdown with sin is carrying the weight of our sins upon our shoulders, as if somehow our guilt or shame will have some redeeming effect on the sin we're in. *It does nothing except condemn us to a less-fulfilled life.* The capacity to redeem sin was given only to

Christ, and he didn't suffer on a cross so we could trudge around in self-condemnation and depression during his perfecting process in our life. God does not want us to carry that kind of load or exemplify that kind of witness. What's more, being convicted about sin doesn't require any feelings of shame or guilt, just the acknowledgment of what we are doing along with the awareness that sin is wrong and there's a better life waiting without it.

> Generally, sin is difficult to stop unless you have something of equal or greater value than the sin itself to replace it with.

Every sin, shortcoming, and breakdown of our human condition was nailed to the cross so we could live in complete freedom; freedom that would bring such rich blessing to our heart, mind, soul, and spirit that the sins we dabble in would eventually lose their allure and go away. In other words, the value of the sins we entertained (whether occasional or perpetual) would pale in comparison to the full experience of what God desires each of us to have in our lives.

In the minutes and hours of *every* day, sin derives its oxygen to stay alive when there is an absence of our communion with God. It is only when we are more aware and filled with his freedom, power, and presence that there will be less room for sin; it becomes a "no vacancy" reality because all the rooms of our mind are filled with the fruit that can come only from a fully engaged relationship with God. When we walk in light we become lighter. *Walk in the full freedom of Christ's perfect and permanent work today.*

The Question: What would my life look like with greater degrees of obedience and fewer strongholds?

4. Reaping Blessing from Adversity

> In contrast to popular thinking, we should lean into adversity, not run from it.

Consider it pure joy, my brothers and sisters, whenever you face trials of many kinds.

James 1:2

When a storm comes, most animals by nature run away from the storm only to be followed by it—remaining wet, uncomfortable, and pushed into potential danger. The buffalo, in contrast, charges into the storm, knowing it will move over them in short order. Sure enough, the storm passes quickly and life for the buffalo resumes its course to focus on other things.

Like the buffalo, when trouble enters our lives we would be best served to run toward the trouble rather than away; embrace it rather than despise it, deal with it rather than delay it, and profit from it rather than fear it. Tragically, the inherent growth God has for us during times of trouble is often missed completely because we spend most of our energy escaping from comfort to comfort instead of seizing the value of this uniquely divine appointment called a trial.

Understanding God's purpose in adversity is the beginning of our wisdom in leveraging value from it and the catalyst to be at peace with an enemy who will never cease. One thing is certain: life is messy. The next trial is just around the corner, and how we hold trials is the game changer to neutralize them into the healthiest possible place.

Those who choose to view a headwind as a soon-to-be tailwind have a different air about them.

This truth remains: God sends or allows headwinds into our lives to build our strength, draw us closer to him, forge closer relationships, and develop our character. Some headwinds are light, some are severe, some contain sand, and other winds seem laden with shards of glass. Not very comforting, yet each wind has intrinsic value regardless of the pain or difficulty it brings.

Unfortunately, when trouble comes, we're usually consumed by the problem, and when the problem becomes the focus, the great work God is doing in the midst of it becomes blurred or vanishes from sight. When we connect to God's promises and see his perfect plan in adversity, we will become clear on how he wants to use us in the trial, which advisors he wants us to engage with for help, and how to access God's strength and wisdom to help leverage the trial into the fullness of what it can be.

One who encounters a problem and holds true to what God says about trials becomes an asset to trial instead of a liability, in turn, controlling the trial in a good way instead of the trial controlling them in a bad way. *Take a trial from an earthly view and put it into a heavenly view today and see what* doesn't *happen.*

The Question: What would it look like to profit from one trial I am currently in, and how might I be used to glorify God in the process?

5. Seizing What Is in Front of You

> Move at the speed of awareness.

In their hearts humans plan their course,
but the LORD establishes their steps.
Proverbs 16:9

Our heart, mind, and eyes work in concert, but our eyes are strategically pointed outward for a reason other than seeing our way around the planet. Connected to the heart and mind, our eyes should be purposed to see the needs of those around us, and yet we can go through life at such a blinding speed that we fail to see the addiction growing, the divorce coming, the business failing, or the relationship struggles with those God has placed around us.

Have you ever considered that your heart, mind, and sight may be moving so quickly that you blaze past all that is rich and in need of your total presence? Perhaps like a film in fast-forward, those around you are not getting the fullness of your love, gifting, or attention; instead they get fragmented frames of your presence, flickering so fast that there's no room for intimacy, impact, or fulfillment . . . let alone memories. As a result, the fabric of rewarding relationships is compromised. This is the pace of many believers. Most times the pace is too fast, other times too slow, and for fleeting moments of beauty, power, and potential, it moves at just the right speed . . . the speed of "awareness."

> I was once asked, "What is your vision for the future, Dean?"
> I replied, "To be present with you, right here, right now.
> That's all that matters . . . and the future looks bright!"

It convicts me when I read of the encounters Jesus had with others in day-to-day life. Although there was great attention on him most times, he remained attuned to what was going on around him despite the intensity and noise of his surroundings. He moved at the pace of presence and awareness. When (amidst the crowd) the bleeding woman simply touched Jesus's garment, he was moving with an awareness and felt the power drain from him (Luke 8:43–48). His agenda was nothing more than to be present—to move at the pace of where external realities could become internal callings, where acknowledging, receiving, and responding were as natural as breathing and as peaceful as resting. And we can be the same way.

> We gain wisdom when we move at a pace
> to see what we would normally miss.

It escapes us at times that God is omnipresent. And although we cannot practice his geographical omnipresence, we can practice the traits of his relational presence everywhere we are. Perhaps we should aspire to simply move at a speed through which we can be uncommonly present and aware with others rather than at the pace of tension-infused agendas. We can trust God to handle our past and our future so present moments can be the gift they were meant to be. *Move at the pace in which great things can happen today.*

The Question: What am I missing by NOT moving in a state of awareness?

6. Releasing Tension with Others

> Life is filled with amazing, weird, abrasive, gentle, controlling, unusual, serious, creative, rigid, casual, analytical, wonderful, intense, and yes, even bizarre people and more.

If it is possible, as far as it depends on you, live at peace with everyone.

Romans 12:18

It wasn't until I was a CEO of a company that I truly understood and valued the diversity in people. Until that point, I had a very difficult time processing the various kinds of personalities that existed in my office, let alone on the planet. It seemed the people I migrated to the most were the ones who were most like me. Anybody who was too far from me in their personality often became a small or large cross to bear, and the relationship suffered through the lens of my self-righteousness and ignorance. As I began to encounter some major challenges in my business and saw clearly how others helped in their own uniqueness and beauty, I started to genuinely appreciate and value the distinct qualities that make up humanity and began to understand the personalities that often accompanied the gifts. Since that time, I've discarded any judgments that I have toward others and believe everyone to be brilliant in their own way; yet if I'm honest, it's still a battle at times to contend with those who are different. I remain guilty of the FACTS below.

> Anyone who looks upon another in judgment knows not who they really are. They invent themselves solely by comparison to others and rarely end up beyond compare.

FACT: There are certain kinds of people who rub you wrong.

FACT: They are not going away, *ever.*

FACT: They are the ones you feel the urge to judge harshly, but rarely (if ever) have the courage to confront OR love.

FACT: Holding others in judgment gives them the keys to drive your emotions, your thoughts, and your life.

FACT: Anyone you judge is a gift to reveal any self-righteousness that lives inside you.

FACT: Wisdom is not found in judging others' differences but in discovering their gifts and seeing their value.

FACT: You need some of what these people have, and they need some of what you have.

If we hold others in a place of judgment, we will miss out on many of the opportunities and pleasant surprises God has in store for us by loving from a sacrificial place. God calls us to love the unlovable, even our enemies. Of course, we can't do this without God's wisdom, strength, discernment, and resolve. But with these things, we can see, access, and draw out the beauty in others, regardless of their "whatever." *Consider loving those who are different or difficult as your biggest opportunity to grow today.*

The Question: What difficult person(s) in my sphere of influence might benefit from me loving them more like Christ?

7. The Infinite Strength Within You

> A new and improved "you" is instant when you receive who you are . . . *in Christ!*

I praise you because I am fearfully and
   wonderfully made;
   your works are wonderful,
   I know that full well.

Psalm 139:14

It seems that many Christians have opted to climb on board the Mediocrity Train: surviving more than thriving, plodding along more than capitalizing on the potential of life, or simply falling short of experiencing all God has for them. The throttle of the Mediocrity Train ranges from being intermittently on to being stuck on full, with the focus more on what we don't have in life rather than on what we do. This causes us to lose strength and lose sight of the many spiritual assets we possess in the present, and we forget the value of who we are now. As you know, once it gets moving, it's not easy to stop a train.

Acknowledging who we are in Christ is the most
powerful knowledge we could ever acquire.

I will hit this principle from different angles because the most
detrimental issue in our desire to become a more fulfilled, joyful,
and effective Christian is "the disconnection" from all the spiritual assets we have in Christ *right now* . . . and there are many.
There are reasons for the detachment. It can be as simple as losing track of who we are in him to willfully ignoring this truth
to stay comfortable—not having to risk in life so we can stay in
control. Fact is, it's easy to maintain control of a life where little
to nothing is happening, but there is little reward in that kind of
control . . . *or life.*

It doesn't take much to get caught in the trap of focusing on
who we are not or *what we don't have* rather than receiving God's
perspective of our beauty, power, and prize, which bolsters our
strength to thrive and take new territory. True strength comes from
accepting that what God says about who we are is true, and operating in that belief—not frantically chasing after spiritual assets we
are deceived into believing we don't have. The best news about the
acceptance of our current capacity in Christ is that it can happen
in a second or two and has the ability to change everything from
the time it takes place.

Staying aware of our God-given inheritance creates a wonderful
space for amazing things to happen, but we often overlook that it
may take effort to get to and stay in that place of awareness. God
calls us to stay focused on who we are in him as a discipline, and
he desires for us to walk in his power perpetually, not just occasionally. It is in this place of awareness where the acknowledgment of
who we *really* are can seep through our busyness, insecurities, and
disbelief and manifest in every thought and action. Think of it
this way: to stay cognizant of God is to know the fullness of God.

How closely we know God will determine how well we know who we are in him. Only then will we embrace the power we already have regardless of where we are in life or what we've attained. *Take ownership of who you are in him in all that you do today.*

The Question: At what level do I own God's many promises about who I already am in him?

8. Modeling Christ to Others

> It is Christlike behavior that can influence others to "look into Christ."

We are therefore Christ's ambassadors, as though God were making his appeal through us. We implore you on Christ's behalf: Be reconciled to God.

2 Corinthians 5:20

As Christians, we have a rather long job description. It's woven throughout the Bible, and there is no shortage of responsibilities, directives, and instruction for our thoughts, way-of-being, and actions. Near the top of that list resides our mandate to "demonstrate to others the love and character of God." We are charged to see our heart and actions minister to the basic needs of others, but also to move past the physical effects into impacting their soul and spirit. Our goal becomes less about impressing others with our actions or theological knowledge and more about leaving others with an impression of Christ that they will never be able to shake. This kind of spirit impact rarely, if ever, comes from just doing things, as much as it does from the heart and motives behind the things we do. It is the Christlike, unconditional love in these things that can arouse others into curiosity about Christ and what makes us different.

If you want to get a clear indication of your witness and a reveal of your love, just look at how people react as you engage with them: there it is.

Today, there will be many opportunities to deliver an example of God's heart and love. During those moments we will either be unconsciously *us*, consciously *Christlike*, or awkwardly bouncing back and forth in between. This Ping-Pong practice of service versus selfishness does nothing more than confuse and add suspicion that our motives are tainted somehow, and today, the tainted-motive meter toward Christians is more acute than ever, especially for younger generations.

If our desire is to be a viable witness for Christ, our actions will go beyond basic obedience and will necessitate an ongoing awareness and practice of being loving, relevant, and valuable to those around us. Reaching the goal will require that we measure the effectiveness of our witness not by our intentions but by the fruit of what shows up in relationship with others.

Love others from God's heart today.

The Question: Am I measuring my witness by things I do or the fruit that shows up from what I do?

9. Living in the Posture to Minister

> Ministry is more who you are
> than what you do.

Now to each one the manifestation of the Spirit is given for
the common good. To one there is given through the Spirit
a message of wisdom, to another a message of knowledge
by means of the same Spirit, to another faith by the same
Spirit, to another gifts of healing by that one Spirit.

1 Corinthians 12:7–9

In light of the gifts we all possess, there is no shortage of how we
can be used by our Lord. A simple look at the world today should
give anyone pause to consider the vast number of ways God's love
and provision could improve where things are headed for many.
And with the diversity of gifts we have been given matched with the
diversity of need both inside the church and out, the opportunities
are limitless. But are we in a state of readiness to minister at all
times, or just at designated times?

If summed up in three words, ministry is simply
awareness, *preparedness*, and *engagement*
. . . anytime, anyplace, with anyone.

I've always been perplexed with the basic view of ministry as something one must get into or sign up for, as opposed to it simply being someone *you are*. A lingering bias implies that if we're not involved in one of the many categories or vocations of the standard ministry pool, then we are not serving the kingdom, and therefore not in ministry. Vocations are nothing more than things we do or responsibilities we have; as such, they can be done out of bondage, obligation, self-aggrandizement, and vain deceit rather than from a pure motive. Ministry conducted from a place of selfish ambition or intention often does more harm than good, and generally the tenure of the initiative or position is short-lived and limited in fulfillment and results.

The subtle transition from ministry turning
to misery is a selfish motive away.

True and lasting ministry—regardless of where it shows up—resides in being Christlike in all aspects of doing the things we do, whether vocations or otherwise. It's about the posture of our hearts being in that special space where the fruit of the Spirit is evident and we count others as more important than ourselves. It's moving in the spirit of authentic giving, where for a time we lose track of our own struggles, shortcomings, fears, and agendas and focus solely on serving others in an exemplary manner . . . *without conditions or expectations in real time*. As we empty ourselves, the presence of Christ's love is experienced by all, tasks are done, and we're refreshed, alive, and ready for what's next. This pure and ready posture of ministry inspires others and serves as an example of what is possible through a heart that is prepared to serve in all circumstances. The ministry of awareness, preparedness, and engagement knows no limits where it can show up, and when it does, life gets amazing instantly. *Be aware and prepared in every conversation and circumstance to minister today.*

The Question: Do I view ministry as a place I go to and/or something I do? Or do I see it as someone I can be, every moment of every day?

10. Leveraging Time and Perspective

> Life's biggest lifeline is when we
> live in God's eternal timeline.

The Lord is my strength and my safe cover. My heart trusts in Him, and I am helped. So my heart is full of joy. I will thank Him with my song.

Psalm 28:7 NLV

It's rarely thought about, but as humans, we exist in two timelines. First is the natural timeline, which gives us an average of seventy-seven years from birth to death; the other timeline we live on is the eternal one. As Christians we were conceived before all time, in God's perfect plan, and are simply living in the process of God's perfect eternity—in, of course, an imperfect world. This provides a valuable paradigm to live from, given we do away with looking at life in years and start embracing that we are already in eternity as our current reality.

Case in point. A while back, I was talking with a friend who was in the middle of a ministry split. He was understandably hurt, angry, and confused. He lamented that the long-standing relationships he had with his friends and ministry partners were over. So I asked him, "As it relates to the future outcome of the relationship with your friends, whose timeline are you living in right now, God's or yours?" He asked for clarification. I said that whenever we believe something is in peril, we have a choice to see it in a natural or spiritual timeline. To see the conflict in our own natural timeline will invent a web of confusion about what will be, how it will affect us, when the trial will end, how bad it will get . . . *and rarely is the outcome close to what we invent.*

> "When you betrayed me I knew we would get past it. I was so grateful I chose not to be bitter toward you in real time, but hold you in reconciliation in God's time."

To see things from this natural place and timeline is a "low faith" disposition that will retain or intensify pessimism toward healing and increase bitterness toward others as we remain in the natural timeline. But to see the relationship as already healed before it actually becomes healed embraces God's timeline of perfection and healing in all things. Living in God's perfect timeline is a divine place of faith and maturity—knowing that although the relationships are not healed at the current time, they are already healed in God's time through the blood of his Son, the omnipotence of his promise, and the completion in eternity. Living life in this posture of faith will position us to bring a peaceful, optimistic, and caring "us" into the healing process at *any time.*

God wants us to live through a spiritual lens and open up our thinking into his realm of thought. There is a freedom of living eternally minded that removes the pressure and constraints of time and creates an endless, limitless space to work within. It's God's space and it's a great place to be. *Hold all things in light of God's perfect eternal timeline today.*

The Question: What unpleasant circumstances can I release from my timeline into God's perfect timeline and, as a result, how will I be different in them?

11. Embracing the Church

> Christians who complain about any
> Christian church, repeat after me:
> "I am the Christian church."

I urge you, brothers and sisters, to watch out for those who
cause divisions and put obstacles in your way that are contrary to the teaching you have learned. Keep away from them.

Romans 16:17

In our "I've got the secret sauce" world, complaining or gossiping
about *our* church, *the* church, or that *other* church has become
sport. It has also become a form of divisiveness based on com-
parative measures that, in the long run, doesn't amount to much
value for those in the church. Those outside the church who hear
this controversial commentary get confused, wondering why there
is such judgment, separatism, and disdain for the difference in
various church denominations by those who proclaim to follow
Jesus Christ, hold the Bible as their sole foundational truth, and
believe in salvation by grace and not works, through the blood
of Christ.

Unfortunately, the Christian church today has become somewhat of a punching bag for many believers who don't obtain the Burger King "Have It Your Way" experience. It's no wonder Christians are coming to church less or leaving it. Some younger Christians are holding the church experience as irrelevant, and many non-Christians are avoiding the pews and seats as if they were covered with anthrax. Many have branded the church as dysfunctional, hopeless, and petty with every flippant, self-righteous comment—all in the name of "I've got it figured out," "I can do it better," or "I'm not that church."

> The only church that doesn't have serious problems is the one you haven't been attending long enough.

The need for diversity in the church stylistically and otherwise is the equivalent to the fact that I hate sardines and others love them. Where some would never go to a church that raises their hands and dances, others wouldn't go if they spoke in tongues, played rock music, or prayed out loud. The nuances are there to serve the body, not for us to sit back and judge simply because it doesn't fit our background, taste, or criteria.

The fact is, we rarely know the full story of any church, so there's no room for piety, arrogance, or judgments about things we know little about. The Bible-believing Christian church is one massive body with millions of members. How we arrived at these denominational, stylistic units is primarily because of a difference of doctrinal opinions, and (in most cases) an insecure need to be right or be different. It's sad, but the subtle to serious divisions that come from this are being kept on life support by those feeling a need to belittle the various denominations and/or styles of the Christian church, when in fact all they are doing is belittling themselves and turning others off while assaulting the brand of

Christianity in the process. *Speak words that bring life into God's church . . . your church, our church, the church today.*

The Question: When conversation goes negative on the church, do I bring a perspective that stops the self-righteousness chatter, or am I a contributor who keeps it going?

12. Living the Fullness of Your Character

> The ongoing quandary of "What should I do?"
> will be answered with ease and wisdom after
> you've decided, "Who am I going to be?"

I meditate on your precepts
and consider your ways.

Psalm 119:15

During our lifetime, we will be faced with the question "What should I do?" thousands of times a year. So the idea of becoming skilled-up on "what to do" in the diverse circumstances of our life makes good sense. But getting good at what to do is a conundrum, as what to do is a different scenario every time; a recurring strategy would be a certain miss due to the dynamic nature of what should be done. That's a mind-full, and the thought of it is enough to have us searching for aspirin, let alone answers.

Consider for a moment that being unclear about what to do in most situations and circumstances is nothing more than a symptom of being unresolved about our character and the stand we have chosen to take at that time. In other words, *what we do* comes from *who we are*, which means that changing the direction of our life is never about changing behaviors as much as it is clarifying who we will be and living in the strength and clarity that comes from being versus doing.

> There's no valor in waking up in the morning to do something: there is in waking up to be Christlike!

When we're unsure of these "being" traits—such as *being* kind, gentle, committed, others-focused, giving, caring, transparent, teachable, straightforward, unconditional, bold, etc.—the "what to do" option pool is not only vast, it's confusing and lacks direction and dependability. Think about what happens when you decide to *be* impatient, selfish, judgmental: the *do* turns to doo-doo real quick. Deciding on your way-of-being in life is foundational to all your action and drives what you will do and how you will go about life with great predictability.

For example, when I am counseling someone and the person asks, "What should I do?" which happens often, I respond with, "Well, let's start with who are you going to be in the situation. In fact, complete this statement: 'In this situation, I will be . . .'" Then I just listen to them outline their character, heart, and way-of-being. The more detailed they are about where they will come from when doing whatever it is they will eventually do or say, the more confident they become. When they're done outlining their ways of being—such as humble, open, attentive, repentant, forgiving—I simply ask, "So what would a humble person in this situation do?" Then, one by one, I address the other traits, asking what an open, attentive, repentant, or forgiving person would do—even how that kind of person would act. Nearly every time they know exactly how they will behave, what they'll do; it's birthed in conviction and almost always a behavior that will generate the best result for all involved. Outcomes to the nth degree will present themselves when we get in the habit of employing the various Christlike ways-of-being to precede every action. It's a habit that will bring an ease and grace to all of life and every relationship in it. *Consider your way-of-being in everything you do today.*

The Question: Am I living in a place of decided ways-of-being, or am I winging it based mostly on how I feel?

13. Seeing Offenses as Beauty

> Being offended shouldn't bother
> you, it should enlighten you.

Great peace have they which love thy law: and nothing
shall offend them.

Psalm 119:165 KJV

Consider for a moment what life would be like knowing that no matter what offense came your way, you would welcome it as an opportunity to show love, compassion, and a bit of conversational creativity. It's hard to imagine, but given we imagine it enough, we may begin to evaluate why we allow ourselves to be spiritually and emotionally affected and in some cases wrecked by others' offensive words or actions.

The only certainty in the nature of offenses is that the next offense is just around the corner. It may be one we've experienced before, a new breed, or a hybrid, but make no mistake, one or several are coming soon in one form or another. It will probably happen today! Since we can never really remove offenses from our life, we can only rethink their effect, value, and purpose in drawing us closer to God and others with resilience that bears witness to God's unshakable love and extraordinary self-control.

> People do not have the power to offend us. We
> choose to let them offend us . . . or not!

Whenever someone says, "I was offended by them," I'm always curious about the nerve(s) that were touched. A bit of inquiry reveals an existing area of weakness, resentment, or area of woundedness that hasn't been dealt with and healed, usually one that's been around for quite some time. In other words, the offense exposed an area of spiritual weakness or hurt that needed to be looked at, dealt with, and eventually overcome. These snapshots we call an *offense* are more of a transformational gift than an inconvenience, and perhaps *thanking* the offender for revealing the offendable spirit might be appropriate and productive—it may even bring more conviction to them than us instinctively offending them back.

Things that touch our nerves, agitate us, and give us grief are simply revelations of undone issues that God will deal with sooner or later, depending on our willingness to lean in and create context for the offense. God wants us to be so steeped in his richness and heavenly perspectives that whatever offenses come our way blow straight through us, filtered through our spirit, leaving only compassion, clarity, and a readiness to engage in reconciliation without the presence of our destructive, immature emotions. In fact, the peak of our spiritual maturity is to experience a sense of burden for the offender instead of getting absorbed in the nature and pain of the attack. Being in this state of grace and awareness will be a healing and refining force to anything that comes our way and will give us a settled confidence when the next offense hits. *Let the next offense minister to you so you can minister to those who offend you.*

The Question: When I think of a recent time when someone offended me, what was my response like? How might I have been able to look at their words or actions as an opportunity for my growth?

14. How Comparison Subverts Relationship

> Comparing ourselves to others is an accelerant to fear and a deterrent to freedom.

Am I now trying to win the approval of human beings, or of God? Or am I trying to please people? If I were still trying to please people, I would not be a servant of Christ.

Galatians 1:10

Early on in my career I joined a Christian CEO forum called Convene. It consisted of successful CEOs with businesses that were fairly mature and Christians who seemed to have it all together. They would meet monthly for a full day and speak into each other's lives on how to build better businesses and glorify God in the process. As a young CEO building a new company and a Christian man who was at the infancy of his commitment to Christ, I was feeling quite nervous about attending the first meeting, so in some ways I was already out of relationship with those in the group by comparison before I got started.

Although there were no apparent signs of super maturity or elite spirituality after the first few meetings, I was still believing they were somehow better or more together than I was. Long story short, it took about six months to figure out that everybody had their own brand of strongholds and issues going on; some were obvious, others not so much, but Adam's nature and humanness were alive and well in the room, universally. I learned that if we spend enough time with people, we become aware that no one has their act together to the level we imagine them to and that we desperately need each other in order to grow and learn. Yet our comparisons, if not dealt with, will keep us from living in the freedom of just being ourselves and being okay with that, while letting others be themselves and being good with that as well.

> We should never let our worth be affected by comparing ourselves to others. To do so would be a "fool-time job."

Comparing ourselves to those we think are more talented, successful, or spiritual than we are isn't just the beginning of relational division, *it's a lie*. Whether we position ourselves higher or lower than others, comparison is a device of the enemy to make us feel unrealistically good or bad about ourselves. In contrast, it's a wise disposition to accept that we are ALL the same in God's eyes and are ALL just a few thoughts or experiences away from flat losing it.

God makes it clear in his Word that we are ALL broken, and although every heart is wicked, mind fallible, and motive questionable, we still tend to place pastors, successful persons, and gifted people on a pedestal so high that mutual relational intimacy doesn't stand a chance. We feel small, we make others too big, and we create a gap that serves no one. We should also consider that comparison to others we regard as higher than we are can be a self-fulfilling prophecy to stay small and sabotage our own potential, and comparison to those we place lower than ourselves creates an excuse to stay arrogant and self-righteous.

Comparison is an attribute of a resigned mind, but those who commit to operate at their God-given potential will not put forth the focus or energy to be comparing themselves to anyone or anything, as they won't have time for those trivialities. *Let yourself and others be beyond compare today and just* be.

The Question: What value and freedom would there be in dropping all my comparisons with others today, and what extra room would I have to think about more relevant matters?

15. Prayer and Specificity

> There is often greater intimacy and attunement in prayers of specificity instead of prayers of casual generalities.

Confess your trespasses to one another, and pray for one another, that you may be healed. The effective, fervent prayer of a righteous man avails much.

James 5:16 NKJV

Prayer is such an ongoing part of our daily routine that becoming casual about it, throwing it on autopilot, and going through the motions may have us check the prayer box as "complete" but we can end up a bit *checked out* in the process.

Prayer goes beyond the words we say. It's not just an opportunity to petition God for requests, but an opportunity to grow into a stronger relationship with him and improve the way in which we communicate with both God and others. Praying can become pretty mechanical; in the same way we comb our hair or brush our teeth, our prayers can become so routine that they bleach out intimacy, cloud spiritual sensitivities, allow for distractions, and make it seem at times that we are praying to a distant or inanimate object instead of our Lord and Savior.

Discovering new words to improve our communication
is a good thing. To discover a new heart behind
the words you use is the real thing.

Take *my* prayers, for example: prayers covering the macro points of my life, glazing over my issues with the same repetitive phrases and speaking in a rhythmic deadness. Those were my prayers for many years—praying where my heart was separated from my words while being semi-attached to what I was praying for and who it was I was praying to. I was caught in such a rush-through, form-based cycle of prayer that even I got tired of hearing myself pray. It was a bad acting job at best, *in public or private*, and I noticed I was praying less often. I would give little thought to what I was praying for and would be more concerned about getting through the prayer than connecting to the heart and cause of detailed request, dialogue, and intimacy with God.

I've come to discover there is serious value in slowing down, giving reverence, and connecting more deeply in our prayers—even spending a moment in advance of them to contemplate what God would have us pray about *specifically*. Specificity in our language is a refining force that slows us down to that fervent state of prayer James talks about—*fervent* meaning with emotional intensity and focus. Praying in the details is a practice that keeps us attuned to the prayer so we can move at a pace of reverence, lucidity, and connectedness to the issues we are praying about, and to our God we are praying to. It is the detail of our prayers that will drive fresh, intimate, meaningful communication with God, while autopilot generalities will usually do nothing more than deaden it and move us to avoid it. There is much to pray

> "Everything as worship" will be the most
> transformational effort you'll make and the
> most rewarding place you'll ever find.

The expansive vision for worship is to hold every action, conversation, interaction, and responsibility as an opportunity to reveal Christ's love, glorify his name, and be in that beautiful place called gratefulness/worship. The norm, however, is that we race through the weekdays and all forms of potential worship get merged into Sunday morning, where we tend to crash into praise in a semi-distracted state. And before we reach a place of full surrender, the music stops and the sermon starts; then into our week we go, only to do it again the following week. To already be in the rhythm of worship during the week will make it possible to enter a praise environment where you can "hit the ground worshiping" and continue it when you leave. There is no place on earth we can be or state we can be in that has more redeeming value than being in the place of gratefulness and worship.

If you want to take a radical leap in your Christian walk, start the journey of being in an ongoing state of worship in all things—to begin everything you do with the question "How can what I'm doing right now be an act of worshiping God?" It is in this state of mindfulness that you begin to experience gratefulness as well as insight and innovation in ALL things: the little things, the difficult things. It is within this attitude that you'll find God's endless well of value, where Christlike behavior becomes as natural as it ever will. *View everything you say and do as an act of worship today.*

The Question: Do I reserve worship, gratefulness, and focused acknowledgment of God for twenty to thirty minutes a week, or can it be a constant state of my mind, heart, and spirit?

17. The Value and Assuredness of Risk

God loves it when we risk.

Immediately Jesus reached out his hand and caught him.
"You of little faith," he said, "why did you doubt?"

Matthew 14:31

If we were to be honest with ourselves, we'd all say we have unmet goals, unfulfilled dreams, and sidelined ministries, visions, and the like. And if we remained in that place of honesty, we'd come clean that some form of fear was in the way of these things getting some field-time in our lives. As a result, life moves quietly to a more riskless, tasteless existence if we allow fear to paralyze us from the value of a good risk.

Knowing God created all people, and knowing our attributes are in his likeness, I have to think that God has great appreciation for when we take risks. I believe it gives God great joy when we put ourselves in a place where we must count on his strength, seek his wisdom, and rely on his comfort. Risk has a built-in intimacy feature that can take us from a stoic-to-average relationship with God and bring us to a place of collaboration and closeness that few other things can—*and do so quickly.*

Risk it, then task it. If you don't, you'll live life in a casket.

So what stops us from this guaranteed intimacy and growth that often leads to some form of achievement and progress? The main factors are the fear of failure, the fear of letting others down, the fear of success, or the hard work that accompanies it. Fear can even manifest in a concern of letting God down. But God isn't disappointed if things go sideways. When they do, he simply uses the experience to build a better us. If we make mistakes, he course-corrects. If we go overboard, he throws a life preserver. God is supportive of whatever he puts on our hearts. But what grieves God more than anything is a life incapacitated by unbelief: a life seeking safety, craving only old experiences while the vision for new experiences becomes more distant and seemingly unattainable. Consider the parable of the talents, where a play-it-safe disposition focused on mitigating risk became revolting in God's eyes. Knowing we serve a no-limits God means we should move toward no-limit thinking, but beyond just thinking, move toward no-limit actions so we can experience the limitless nature of God's provision.

Digging ourselves out of any ruts of limitation is as easy as acting on the following question: "What is it that I believe God wants me *to do*—but I need to be in deeper relationship with him *to actually do it*—that perhaps I've been unwilling *to do*?" Identify that, and step into it with the assurance that God will do nothing short of a miraculous work in your life, whether you succeed at "the thing" or not. *Step into a risk you've been unwilling to take and invite God into the journey with you today.*

The Question: Do I place more value on staying in control of a small game or is there a bigger, better, brighter future where the only option is to risk so I must count on God's strength?

18. Resilience in the Face of Betrayal

> When someone does something to betray us, it's wise to consider who is really responsible for the sin.

Above all, love each other deeply, because love covers over a multitude of sins.

1 Peter 4:8

Chances are someone will betray you before a month passes. Some acts will be overt; others will take place in their mind. Knowing the sheer number of betrayals that will be perpetrated against us, it stands to reason we would turn pro at dealing with these hurts, deceptions, and offenses, keeping our grace and wisdom elevated while minimizing our judgments and stress levels.

The sins of man are as the hands of time—never stopping and seemingly more active as time moves on. The Bible speaks of increased acts of sin as end-times draw near, and we should be aware that more of these sins will land on us with greater frequency and intensity. We will experience acts of treachery, violence, deceit, lies, affairs, thievery, and many more. But how we hold those sins and those who sin against us will be the deciding factor in sustaining the fruit of the Spirit in our life and how we will be used to war against that sin.

> Judging others who sin against you doesn't
> elevate you, it separates you.

I'm pretty sure when Jesus turned over the tables in the temple, his anger wasn't directed solely at the sinner, but at the sin, the author of that sin, and what those in the temple were missing by living a life of greed and lack of reverence. This is my assertion, of course, but for us to look past the friend, relative, or stranger who sinned against us and know who the true enemy is—Satan—will put us in a unique position to be something other than wrapped up in the emotions of a betrayal, positioning us as a warrior to do battle with the appropriate enemy. By exercising empathy, discernment, and a loving approach to the sinner, we get to move to a new level of self-control, where sins against us are held smaller and less significant compared to God's perfect work, demanding less from our emotions and having less impact on our fulfillment or service to others.

With a clear understanding of who the culprit for sin really is, we will see the potential of others in Christ. We may even be used to exemplify God's enduring grace and mercy, calmly bringing the sinner to recognition of the ramifications of their behavior— recognition that could never manifest if we were judging, condemning, and owned by bitterness and resentment. *Don't make the sinner pay today; make the* author of sin *pay today.*

The Question: When someone sins against me, am I prepared to extend grace, love, and truth to the person while engaging in battle with the real enemy?

19. Accessing More Power to Thrive

> Taking new ground in your life without improving your relationship with God is like climbing a higher mountain and using that old climbing rope . . . *Don't fall for it.*

The Sovereign LORD is my strength;
   he makes my feet like the feet of a deer,
   he enables me to tread on the heights.
Habakkuk 3:19

In life, we will experience many new phases of growth, visions, goals, and dreams. We could be starting a new business, relationship, ministry calling, or passion—*anything, really.* Typically these endeavors start off with a great deal of enthusiasm only to be confronted with real or imagined obstacles inherent in building something new. But the real problem with taking new ground is not the expected pool of obstacles, the newness, and the unknowns; the biggest liability is that we don't take the time to examine whether our current relationship with God is robust enough for the advance.

A new vision will always require more strength and resolve than we had before and will stretch our capacity to the point where the need for elevated and sustainable spiritual strengths are required to stay in the game, let alone thrive in it. A quick glance at our current relationship with God may reveal our time in the Word is fragmented, our conversations with God are becoming recycled and mechanical, and/or our acuity to access and engage with the Spirit of God is dull and in need of sharpening. It may be that the old habits and disciplines that helped us get by in previous times won't stand a chance against the new adventure with all its challenges and a relentless enemy who doesn't want to see it happen.

Taking new ground in our lives will require
we get grounded in new things.

To sustain the intensity of taking new ground, our spiritual disciplines and our intimacy with God would benefit from moving to a new commitment. The question is, "Is my current intimacy with God strong enough for where I am, and will I bring it to a new level for the places I'm going?" The truth is, we can confidently enter into any new vision as long as our relationship with God is aligned to the advance. *Make the choice today to move your relationship with God to a level that matches what's next.*

The Question: What could a new standard in my relationship with God look like—tangibly, specifically, daily?

20. The Value of Inquiry

> Did you know it's physically impossible to
> be angry and curious at the same time?

> My dear brothers and sisters, take note of this: Everyone
> should be quick to listen, slow to speak and slow to become
> angry, because human anger does not produce the righ-
> teousness that God desires.
>
> James 1:19–20

When things get heated in conflict, it helps the situation to calm our nerves, de-stress the environment, and address others with calm, Christlike behavior—to manage the tension and usher in a safe place for restoration to begin.

So what's the silver bullet to deal with conflict most effectively and efficiently? One word—*curiosity*: a discovery into the root of our own behavior and the realities and emotional needs of others. The moment we become inquisitive about our own behavior in a conflict is the moment the emotional valve that releases anger slams shut, and the moment we stop being inquisitive is about the time a mild-to-wild flow of anger, judgment, and blame shows up.

We can get into such a committed state of curiosity that we actually become fascinated by the nature of the conflict and desire to do nothing more than to get to the root of the issue, whether we are at fault or not. This creates a heightened sense of awareness and personal accountability that has remarkable impact on current and future conflicts. When others know that we're willing to be curious and account for our behaviors, it creates a safe place for them to become open about their role and neutralizes the toxic emotions that can escalate the conflict far beyond what it should ever become. It comes down to this: it's never the conflict that matters, but the restraint and maturity we bring to the conflict that makes the difference. This should be the focus. Great things happen in restraint and inquiry.

> The creativity of your questions will drive
> the trajectory of your conversations.

It's always good to be curious about the conflict immediately, looking first to what the needs of the other person are within the conflict and then asking ourselves how we may have allowed or contributed to the problem. It's that "serve others first, account for our own actions" approach that is the way of the Lord—not the "I'm the victim" stance we often take. Curious, or angry? Given it's one or the other, I'll take curious anytime . . . and so will others, gratefully. *Don't perspire in conflict; inquire in conflict and steward over the breakdown today.*

The Question: In what conflict or breakdown could I test a bit of humble curiosity?

21. Loving Others versus Impressing Them

> The greatest indication of our theological acumen will be revealed in the ways we love others.

> If I have the gift of prophecy and can fathom all mysteries and all knowledge, and if I have a faith that can move mountains, but do not have love, I am nothing.
>
> 1 Corinthians 13:2

Over the years, I've found myself in the company of some great theologians: people who can draw and shoot out a Scripture faster than Billy the Kid. Some of these theologians were humble and kept their comments holstered until the appropriate time, while the overzealous ones kept shooting off their theological knowledge and concepts, hitting everyone in their path with little consideration of relevance or impact. There was always an odd pressure for them to impress you with their knowledge, and they made sure you knew you were an infidel if you veered off *their* interpretation of

Scripture in the slightest. Candidly, they were the kind of people who brighten a room by leaving it. Despite all of their knowledge, a few essentials were missing from their theological strength: discernment, restraint, and most of all, *love*.

> Whoever said that knowledge is the key to life
> knows little of love and even less about life.

Every strength we possess is a weakness if it goes too far. Artful communication is great until it talks too much; listening is awesome until you stop sharing what's on *your heart*; the ability to control things is great until you become a control freak; and theological acumen is great until it becomes self-righteous, absent of love and sensitivity. For example, I've seen people become so intent on learning God's Word for reasons of self that not enough attention was paid to family relationships—and those relationships became a train wreck. God did not give us his Word to be used as an escape from our core responsibilities as a Christian, but to improve them.

There are thousands of details in Scripture with the nuances of Greek and Hebrew, various translations, and interpretations; so much so that a lifetime could be spent studying Scripture and God's ways would still be higher than the heavens. Don't get me wrong, getting schooled up in the Word is a foundational need for every Christian. However, every Scripture in the Bible is designed to support and improve our attempts to live out the following mandate: love the Lord with all your heart, soul, mind, and strength as the first and greatest commandment, and love your neighbor as yourself. On these two commandments hang ALL the Law and the Prophets (see Matt. 22:37–40). God narrows all commandments and theology down to these two simple things, and he wants every page read, prayer said, and act of worship lifted up to revolve around fulfilling them. He also wants us to measure the effectiveness of this call by the results we see showing up in our life and the lives of others, not by how well we think we are doing using self-evaluation. They are simple commandments in their makeup, but difficult in execution.

The world today is not moved by our ability to pull out a Scripture at will; they are intrigued when they see the resolve of a grounded human being, unshaken by earthly circumstances, living in a state of peace and joy and loving others with consistency and extravagance. We would be wise to remember this as we read God's Word. *Let what you read in his Word drive love, intimacy, and humility into every thought and action.*

The Question: Is learning God's Word driving me to love God and others more richly or fueling a need for me to be more impressive?

22. The Reality of Our Physicality

Where does physical health meet
spiritual strength? *Here's the skinny!*

Therefore, whether you eat or drink, or whatever you do, do
all to the glory of God.

1 Corinthians 10:31 NKJV

In biblical times, there wasn't room for physical atrophy or a poor
diet. You had to walk everywhere and work the land, and the only
fast food around was when you accidentally inhaled a fly. The
Bible doesn't offer a great deal on the topic other than at the fall
of mankind, our bodies began to deteriorate, that we should take
care of our temples, and that gluttony kills . . . *all wise to note.*

Today's fast-food world of minimal physical activity offers a
great opportunity to evaluate how our physical condition affects
our capacity to serve God and others. Although the old saying that
"the world goes to the energetic" is not entirely true, I began to
wonder what all the spiritual gifts, talents, and callings fueled by
limited physical energy were doing, how little they were doing, and
(frankly) if they were doing anything at all. I thought about how

71

all these abilities were immobilized by mental fogginess, limited stamina, and a tired commitment.

Standing to lose a few pounds myself forced me to consider what those in *my* life were missing while I droned around in a food coma. My wife, family, employees, clients, friends, and ministry partners were all experiencing a groggy, inconsistent, semi-alert, half-committed "me." So I changed my diet, dropped twenty pounds, and am grateful I took the steps . . . as are others, especially my wife. If we really took to heart the call that God has on our life and considered the needs of those around us, we would be more serious about what we put into our bodies and how we treat them. For when God says, "Go ye therefore," he wants us in great spiritual condition. He wants us to have the physical strength for the journey ahead and the ability to go far if he calls for that.

It's no accident the word *die* is in *diet*. We must kill off our addiction to food to live in the fullness of life.

Another part of health/spirituality stewardship shows up in the duration of our life. Based on what I've read and seen with my own eyes, I estimate that most who ignore their health shave five to thirty years off their life. It's a little known fact that on average, Christians hit the peak of their spiritual maturity and effectiveness between fifty-five and sixty-five. So it's safe to say that if premature death occurs because we choose an unhealthy lifestyle, ten to twenty years of high-impact kingdom opportunities may be lost. Add to that the incapacitating effects of illness and the burden multiplies, not just with us and those we care about; we actually pull others out of their life and calling as well, as they must sideline their life to care for our dwindling health. This is not a health epidemic; it is a spiritual pandemic of selfishness, gluttony, laziness, and resignation. Tough words, yes, but to soften them would be a disservice. Individual lives and relationships depend on it, as does the potential of our service to God! *Eat well and see how you think, feel, act, and sleep today.*

The Question: Am I stewarding my health for maximum kingdom impact, blessing, and fullness of life, or am I living in physical deficiency and coping with it by calling it normal?

23. Maximizing Your Gifts

> Everyone has gifts. Not everyone
> chooses to strengthen their gifts.

Just as a body, though one, has many parts, but all its many
parts form one body, so it is with Christ.

1 Corinthians 12:12

I'm always amazed at the unique gifts and abilities I encounter from
those I meet in life. In fact, the more I appreciate the differentiating
qualities of others' gifts, the more resolved and confident I become
in my own. I don't say this from an egocentric standpoint but from
gratefulness for what I do have while being genuinely content with
what I don't. In Christ, we are collectively one body, all serving
with different attributes, which removes the potential arrogance
or shortsightedness of weighing one gift over the other. We are all
created equally different yet uniquely brilliant with some common
threads here and there.

One who is operating in the fullness of
their gifts leaves less room in their life for
stress, annoyances, and negativity.

It's reassuring to know that God has given each of us a specific gift or gifts to impact others, to bring glory to God, and to enjoy the fruit of all he bears through us. He knew that in the difficulty of life itself, sharing ourselves from our unique gifting would be one of the predictable sustainers of our joy—a place where we could meet God in ongoing victory. Although there is no doubt that each of us has something extraordinary to give, some of our gifts are flourishing, others are limping along, some remain dormant, and some gifting is buried deep in limiting beliefs or complacency.

God hardwires these gifts in us at spiritual birth, so obviously they start off as infantile, while the potential of their strength, reach, and influence is nothing short of miraculous. Yet many gifts sit on the shelves of our heart collecting dust and getting little or no use because those who possess them are inexperienced and lacking the confidence needed to pull them off that shelf and put them into life. The potential of any gift lies in wait per our commitment to learn about it, strengthen it, and perfect it through use—while interacting with the Holy Spirit in its practice.

There are many things we can do that bring value to our Christian experience and create more intimacy with God. Exercising our gifts is among *the* most valuable. The simple process of bringing our gifts to life builds our confidence and character quickly and efficiently, and brings a balance to life that levels out the peaks and valleys of living. God has a way of honoring our service, not just in the work he does through us but in what he builds into us in the process—these are the gifts within the gift, and there are many. *Contemplate some ways you can strengthen the brilliant gifts you have today.*

The Question: What specific things can I do, who should I connect with, and who needs my gifts so I can move my strengths to a new level?

24. Communicating to Resonate

> A little consideration in the words we use and how we say them will determine if they reach the ears, mind, heart, and spirit or just the air.

To the weak I became weak, to win the weak. I have become all things to all people so that by all possible means I might save some.

1 Corinthians 9:22

Knowing that God spoke life and all existence into creation out loud is a clear indication that God values the language of words. As humans we value them as well; life's natural progress is driven through conversations, the words we use, and the ways in which we choose to deliver them. Now consider that our witness to others is often measured by the words we share, and how words hold a power that should never be taken lightly.

So if all of life and death exists in the power of the tongue, why is there so little emphasis from the pulpit today on how to effectively communicate and resonate with others? One reason is found in the arrogant assumption of, *if I speak, others should listen . . . they owe it to me to listen.* It's a pretty useless assumption considering all the factors we bring into communication.

When broken down into parts such as body language, position, tone, volume, enunciation, facial expression, attitude, pace, rhythm, and oh, I almost forgot, the words themselves and the heart behind them, we begin to see there are quite a few things to consider to get a message across the way we intend. The result of ignoring the details in communication is that much of what we say to others will land on deaf ears, and any future attempts to communicate them will be filtered through the lens of that last experience. Not the kind of conversational or relational momentum we want.

Everyone receives communication differently. It is wise to consider what will resonate before a single word is spoken.

The apostle Paul was perhaps the most brilliant man of his time. With his ability and intelligence, you'd think if he showed up to a meeting people would listen. *And they did.* Not because he was brilliant or a great speaker, but because he was wise and relatable. I believe Paul invested forethought prior to conversations and gatherings and was considerate in preparing his approach so nothing would distract or prevent people from paying attention to his words. He adapted his content according to the type of crowd he'd be speaking to and most likely altered his communication style—even his attire—to ensure those he was with would be spoken to in a way that ministered to them. Paul was about connection, creating trust, and valuing others as the precedent for every encounter. It was the best chance of people feeling valued, respected, and open to listening to something new.

There is great wisdom in discerning how best to communicate, and the Holy Spirit is always available for collaboration. It's the time you'll spend before any conversation, meeting, or gathering that will determine whether the after*math* adds, subtracts, multiplies, or divides. *Communicate in a way that relates to your audience today.*

The Question: When I speak, do I do it more to feel good about what I say, or do I consider how best I may be heard?

25. Living in the Now

> Stay in the present where God
> stays: *the omnipresent.*

The LORD has done it this very day;
let us rejoice today and be glad.
Psalm 118:24

There is a sacred place on earth that houses more peace and joy
than any other place; that place is where you are in the moment—
the present, the here, the *right now*. However, our inventions of
what *may* soon happen, how things or life *may* end up can rob
our present and the peace and joy God intended.

If you contemplate past what I call general lifestyle challenges,
you may remember a whole host of mental inventions about how
bad it was, what might happen, how your image might be affected,
and on and on. And yet you got through it. Although it may have
been very hard at the time, it was mostly the anxious invention of
present and future repercussions that interrupted God's flow of
beauty and perfection in the now. And while our physical bodies
can never actually escape a present moment, our mind can travel

so far into mental inventions that by the time we get back to God's reality about what is true, the day and all the opportunities in it are gone and we feel less connected to what may have been possible.

> Life unfolds. We should move at the pace of life and not allow mental inventions to interrupt that natural unfolding.

The practice (more often, habit) of living in the realm of "what might happen" generally erases fulfillment from everything and everyone in the present. The ability to live fully content in present moments is a testament to the quality of our faith and the maturity of our walk. It reveals our trust in God to take care of future things so we don't bring the weight and heaviness of tomorrow (or a year or ten years) into today. Today has enough weight of its own, and it would serve us well to travel a bit lighter on the journey of life. Consider the value of focusing on thriving in the minutes and don't jump ahead into the days, weeks, and months that are impossible to experience in their fullness until we are living them.

There is amazing freshness and soberness that rests on people who choose to live in the present, which has us seeking their company and inquiring of their counsel. I imagine the commentary from most Christians who live this way would be profoundly simple: "I hang out where God hangs out: in the present. I move at the pace of God's time and press the stop, pause, and play buttons instead of the fast-forward button. I find everything I need is right here in these moments and nowhere else. Care to join me?" *Replace thoughts about the future with thoughts that have value in present moments today.*

The Question: Would others say I stay present in the moment, or do they see me worrying about the future, drifting from the now?

26. Solving Arguments Before They Begin

> Arguments don't manifest from the outside in, but the inside out.

What causes fights and quarrels among you? Don't they come from your desires that battle within you?

James 4:1

I would say no one likes to argue, but that's not entirely true. Some argue so they can be right, as their identity is wrapped up in never being wrong. Others do it for sport, because for some reason winning takes precedence over intimacy and a better relationship. Then there's the rest of us who from time to time end up in disagreements with others where emotions get triggered and an argument seems to be the only way to resolve things. But what if there was no such thing as an argument . . . the kind where toxic emotions show up and do more harm than good? What would that say about our need to engage in something that may not exist—knowing it's on us if we choose to bring our internal dysfunctions into issues to satisfy selfish needs rather than communicating responsibly about them from a place of peace, clarity, and love that counts the other as more important than ourselves? *What a concept.*

Fact is, although arguments seem to be going on just about everywhere, you could examine the entire planet with a microscope and never find an argument. Arguments don't exist on earth . . . *anywhere.* They don't come from circumstances or situations; they live inside in our hearts and—in their purest form—are a sign of selfishness, unresolved anger, undone bitterness, and immaturity. In many ways, they are an indication of our general spiritual condition. In other words, an argument is not a thing but a predisposition; it is not an activity but a condition of the heart and mind. With a quick change of our disposition, a heated disagreement can turn to a loving conversation if the argumentative spirit is removed from our hearts. It's no surprise that more life-giving things are said when a person prepares their heart, so the heart drives the content, language, and outcome.

In conflict, it's always better to consider inquiring, not manipulating; relating, not emoting; giving, not taking; accounting, not blaming; and empathizing, not judging.

By staying aligned to God's Spirit, we can push out immaturities and emotional instability and operate with a calming presence and caring heart; we become an instrument of healing and guidance in disagreement, not an instrument of judgment, insecurity, and destruction. I was quite relieved to discover there were no arguments in this world. The fact that they are inside of us gives me hope and a sense of responsibility to improve my "A" game. I realize that a potential argument can be used to glorify God through restraint, self-control, and love.

Given that we do occasionally end up in a blowup of sorts (and we will), it's healthy to realize that in and of themselves arguments aren't bad. We should be grateful when they show up, as they are one of the clearest indicators of the emotional and relational deficiencies we need to work on as well as life issues in need of resolution. They also draw out the things we tend to bury, so we can work through those hidden strongholds that can build up into a number of relational disconnects over time. A good goal for any Christian is to remain free of an argumentative spirit and a posture of being easily offended. Deciding on a godly stance before engaging in any potential conflict will provide a safe place where core honesty is revealed and goes deeper into the place where conflict truly gets resolved. *Be a resource of healing in any and all issues that arise today.*

The Question: Am I more about winning in relationships or winning arguments?

27. The Brand of Christianity

> To the world, Christianity is a brand
> and you are its representative.

Now then, we are ambassadors for Christ, as though God
were pleading through us: we implore you on Christ's behalf,
be reconciled to God.

2 Corinthians 5:20 NKJV

Despite how theologically incorrect the headline reads, the secular world views Christianity as a brand just as they view Apple, BMW, Nike, and others. They judge, compare, and consider it against the beliefs they were raised with, the available religions outside of the Christian faith, and some of the more abstract concepts found in books such as *The Secret*. Anyone starting to look at Christianity will begin to compare the various options crossing their path or vying for their attention, which makes the whole process pretty confusing for the unbeliever. But one fact remains: along the journey of their life, part of their evaluation of Christianity will be based on the true definition of a brand, which is the "total combined experience" that an organization and its people deliver to their intended audience. The intended audience of Christianity happens to include everyone on the planet who is a nonbeliever, and there are many. The other audience is the believer, so the audience of the brand is everyone.

A brand is comprised of a set of values: core
values, valuing others, and delivering value.

As part of the body, every day your own personal brand of Christianity speaks boldly of your intentions to everyone you touch. In fact, your representation or "re-presentation" of your faith never stops affecting others, good or bad. It can't. Even when our brand isn't speaking, it says something about us. *Complacency, perhaps.* Your representation is a constant witness to everyone around you. But what is your brand saying? Is it saying selfish *or* giving, detached *or* intimate, superficial *or* authentic, spineless *or* courageous, consistent *or* inconsistent, prideful *or* humble, semi-committed *or* fully engaged? These are only a few of the many indicators of how we are living out our Christianity, and they are the primary lens nonbelievers look through when they set their sights on eternal things.

God chose us to represent the brand of Christianity here on earth to all who would hear. Although it's the Holy Spirit who draws people to God, God has called us to be a good witness for a purpose. He desires us to be an example of his love to give people a clear understanding of who God is, what a life with him looks and feels like, and what the hope of eternity bears. Because of that, we have a great responsibility to bring truth, integrity, and exemplary execution in all we do while representing the Lord. And in our world, our representation will take place in the moments of our interactions with all people via our attitude, words, and actions down to the nuances of the presence we carry. *Consider the brand of Christianity you are to others today.*

The Question: Knowing my brand of Christianity is among many choices, am I representing a brand that is magnetic or a brand that is apathetic, or worse?

28. Authentic Spiritual Warfare?

> Spiritual warfare is fought on the
> battleground of your mind.

We demolish arguments and every pretension that sets itself
up against the knowledge of God, and we take captive every
thought to make it obedient to Christ.

2 Corinthians 10:5

One of the harder areas of my life to discern is the distinction
between spiritual warfare and anything else that might resemble
it. Due to the fall of humankind and a sin-filled world, I'm forced
to look at everything that happens, such as catastrophe, disease,
tragedy, financial ruin, and death, as nothing more than life itself.
It would be easy to categorize these as spiritual warfare, but some
of these things are self-inflicted and other things happen with a
randomness that defies logic. To think the enemy ordained things
such as mentioned would give Satan a power that he just does not
have. Satan deals within the confines of our mind and capitalizes
when we are in a time or season lacking in spiritual groundedness.
Although that doesn't seem like a great deal of potency, it connects

to how we view everything that happens to us whether real or imagined, and its effects on our life are profound and shouldn't be taken lightly—after all . . . God calls it warfare for a reason.

Spiritual warfare isn't something bad that happens to us. *That's called life in a fallen world.* Spiritual warfare is a mind game of the enemy that occurs before, during, or after something has happened. In other words, it is not the event but how we relate to it that makes way for either spiritual warfare *or* faith. We choose *who* wins that battle. We govern our thoughts, and the moment we relinquish that truth is the moment Satan begins to make stubbing your toe seem like a major life crisis.

Think about it: God's lens calls us to see death as gain, trials as joy, deserts as healing, suffering as strength, and challenges as growth. This is "battleground faith" and the beginning of a spiritually solid life perspective—one that beats the mind games of the enemy into submission and brings the day-to-day life stress we experience to manageable levels. Warfare's reverberation rests largely on whether we truly believe what God says about the value of trials and his perfect plan in allowing or engineering them for our good.

"Dear friends, do not be surprised at the fiery ordeal that has come on you to test you, as though something strange were happening to you. But rejoice inasmuch as you participate in the sufferings of Christ, so that you may be overjoyed when his glory is revealed" (1 Peter 4:12–13).

I've seen many Christians remain stuck, claiming that certain events and outcomes in their life are spiritual warfare, when they need look no further than the mirror to understand that it's not warfare but how they are viewing circumstances and their disbelief in the value of trials that ultimately wreaks havoc with their lives. Sometimes things are labeled as spiritual warfare as a means to escape our own responsibility and governing over the challenges of our life no matter how difficult they are. Even though life issues may be as intense as death and disease, we are always called to a more divine view of these things than the world. The good news is, we can be a great example to others when we stand faithfully in the face of adversity. And while we exemplify an uncommon peace, poise, and healthy perspective, there may be some involved in the trial who have their minds immersed so deeply into the problem that they have no choice but to look for help . . . and there you are, grounded and postured to serve. *Hold adversity in a way that brings life to you and others today.*

The Question: Knowing life will keep throwing curveballs, what am I doing to equip my mind to hold them as opportunity instead of catastrophe?

29. Creating Community at Church

> The equity in our intimacy with others is found in small investments of risk.

Be devoted to one another in love. Honor one another above yourselves.

Romans 12:10

One of the surprising realities inside the Christian church is the amount of loneliness that exists. It really doesn't belong there, and yet loneliness is present in a large percentage of congregations. Over the years I've heard statements like, "We really don't have any couples we spend regular time with," "I don't have anyone I can share my heart with," "It would be nice if there were others that enjoyed the same things we do," and "I don't have anyone to be accountable to." The list goes on, and the reason for it is simple— a fear or unwillingness to step into a journey called fellowship.

Whether you attend a small church, midsize church, or megachurch, the sanctuary, hallways, and congregating areas of the church are filled with people who are choosing loneliness over community—where the focus is more on self than on others, and what might be possible through small, persistent efforts toward relationship. It stems from skepticism about what could happen in and through us as well as what God could usher in if we pushed past the minor discomforts of interaction.

It's amazing how engaged others at church have become with me since I chose to become more engaged with them.

Do a little digging and you'll discover that those who profess loneliness say they are more comfortable to slip in without notice and slip out once the service is complete rather than engaging with others, so any connection is relegated to luck instead of choice. Others become a victim of their own inactivity; waiting to be noticed and approached by someone takes precedence over an opportunity to extend a hand, introduce themselves, or share a kind word. We all struggle from disconnecting from time to time, but even if these brief encounters last but a moment, a series of these small but consistent connections can add a sense of community during a church experience and begin to create opportunities for relationship. But realistically, to expect that lasting community can be built within the service time is similar to the expectation that a full meal can be experienced by eating a single French fry. *Pretty unlikely.*

Over the years, I've discovered that one simple but intentional conversation can cause great things to happen. After some small talk, ask, "Hey, would you like to grab coffee, breakfast, or lunch sometime? It would be great to get to know you." Then follow through on it. Although I'm a quasi-functioning introvert, I've done this many times, never quite knowing the outcome of the meeting but always knowing that God would honor the risk, *and he does.* I've never been rejected in those attempts at connection, and once a relationship moves to a new level of intimacy, it rarely returns to its original form. If stepping out at that level seems too much (which it can at times), volunteering at events, serving in a ministry, and helping where there are other people of similar interests will combat any loneliness or disconnect one might feel at church. We shouldn't feel anything other than community within our churches; we'll receive exactly what effort we put into it, meaning it's never the church that's the problem or the solution, but us. *Move just a little past the average commitment to create new community at church this week.*

The Question: Is there greater possibility for community in my church? Who will I connect with this week?

30. Thinking Deeply for a Change

> Should you meditate? Perhaps you should *meditate* on that for a moment and see what comes up.

Be diligent in these matters; give yourself wholly to them, so that everyone may see your progress.

1 Timothy 4:15

Life is a powerful force. If we succumb to its pace, it will swoop us up and carry us into the stress and confusion of its flow without bias or intent. Once in that flow, much of our precious bandwidth to contend with the more important parts of our life is used up, leaving us frustrated, exhausted, and scrambling to escape. And yet as a believer, every circumstance is minimized to disrupt life if we use our mind in the capacity that God intended. Our mind can either be a factory of affliction or a laboratory to leverage the perspective we need to stay kingdom minded in all things. But using our minds to this degree is seldom exercised because the meditation option God avails to us is rarely exercised. The good news is we can choose to slow down and take a ten-minute (or less) mini-vacation from life to see what God can do with our minds in a still, quiet place of deep, committed thought.

It's astonishing how much better, faster, and easier good things happen since I've slowed down to collaborate with God on how they can happen.

Most of our thoughts on issues that need attention however, are an unplanned series of what I call "inch-deep thoughts" that are generally ineffective due to distractions, so they fail to reach the depth of revelation needed for a godly perspective. These fragments of thought usually take place at the most inopportune times, not giving us the space to process them into resolution. As a result, this habit of surface thinking compounds into an inventory of incomplete thoughts based mainly on our past experiences and feelings, so we miss the value of reengineering those thoughts into something new through meditation. The gold, however, will exist with near certainty in a single, more committed deep dig. Quiet space allows thoughts to be explored with a mind free of debris, while God's thoughts are able to be revived or received at a deeper, more clarified and refined level.

When God tells us that meditation is a process for deep spiritual growth, he is exhorting us to capitalize on the value of this elusive practice relegated mostly to monks and priests. If meditation is seen in this biased light, we will always view it as unrealistic, unattainable, and not the available practice it is. A more pragmatic and approachable definition of *meditate* is simply to think deeply, to picture in one's mind, and to ponder and work through something. There's nothing in that definition that implies sitting on a rug for three hours on a mountaintop in some contrived position to get results.

We can think deeply and effectively about something in a few minutes' time. Almost any place will work for this if we invest ourselves into and practice the process. It is in these purposed moments of intensified thinking where our minds have the time and space to clarify and innovate at much deeper levels. *Take three to five minutes and meditate on what this could mean to your life today.*

The Question: What one issue, challenge, opportunity, or relationship could benefit from some meditation today?

31. The Insanity and Vanity of Profanity

> Profanity is nothing more than a momentary lapse in conversational creativity.

The soothing tongue is a tree of life,
   but a perverse tongue crushes the spirit.

Proverbs 15:4

Go back fifty years and rarely, if ever, would one hear a curse word on the radio, TV, or even a stage. Profanity didn't show up in most conversations, and when it did it was heard like screeching nails on a chalkboard. Today, it seems to be gaining momentum to be more widely accepted in culture, even in the church. We hear "It's not the words I use but the heart in which they are said" as justification. True, motive is important, but the witness profanity reveals and what we miss in terms of bettering our communication leaves room for a cursory look.

Profanity is used in a multitude of ways. Sometimes we use it to relieve stress or make us feel more in control of a situation, conversation, or person. Mostly it's used to emphasize points;

to imbed more intensity or impact into our communication. We mostly use profanity in conversation as a tool to accentuate. The unfortunate aspect of profanity is it generally shows up in the most emotional, opportune parts of a conversation—a time when life or death can be brought forth in the power of the tongue. It's in these moments that we're faced with a powerful growth opportunity: default to profanity or innovate creative content that has greater value and impact than a few expletives. We have an opportunity every time we are tempted to use profanity to reinvent (in real time) the way we communicate, stretching ourselves to become a more creative conversationalist and a better communicator while keeping our character intact.

> More often in conversation, swearing distracts
> people from seeing the truth. And sometimes
> the words we don't say make a bigger statement
> about our character than ones we do.

Due to the emotions we feel when doing it, we may think profanity opens up and awakens, but really, it closes minds, shuts down opportunity, bears poor witness, and (in a subversive manner) makes *us* feel and look smaller and less intelligent. It puts our faith in delivering expletives rather than in what God could do if we struggled in the refrain and exercised our minds to make more powerful, poignant statements. Consider this a discipline to develop your character and creativity and to better all communications. Consider this an option that God will honor and replace with something far more rewarding and progressive than a split second of feel-good indignity. *Avoid the curse today.*

The Question: In what ways do I use profanity, and how have I rationalized its presence in my life?

32. Being Used to Alleviate Despair

> If you want to help someone who is heading toward a fall, sensitivity with intentionality will serve well.

Brethren, even if anyone is caught in any trespass, you who are spiritual, restore such a one in a spirit of gentleness; each one looking to yourself, so that you too will not be tempted.

Galatians 6:1 NASB

Being used by God to help stop the flow of despair or an eventual crash in someone's life isn't light fare. The flow is generally strong, the currents are treacherous, and the waters are tricky and tough to navigate. Going into it with a casual posture is certain to get all concerned into deeper, more dangerous waters while putting the relationships involved at risk. Whether gifted or not, however, we are all called to this work, so approaching it with the right heart and an engaged stance with the Holy Spirit can have profound results, even if our skill level isn't where we think it needs to be. In fact, some of the most transformational moments of making a difference have been facilitated by someone who had the right heart rather than refined skill.

A person who makes a constant difference in the lives of others is a sowing machine. In turn, they become a reaping machine. ☺

The process of this delicate work begins by stepping into risk and addressing the problem, not by condemning the person. When we work with someone in a "making a difference" capacity, we should start by initiating loving inquiry and listening, *not by launching a bombastic inquisition*. This allows us to operate from a place of empathy and will give us more insight into how best to serve and create a safe place for truth to be shared. Once we understand the nature of the breakdown, our goal is to lovingly help with what's not working by providing perspectives or encouragement, and if we can't offer viable feedback, to consider connecting the person to someone who can (with their permission, of course). To make progress, the foundation of this delicate work must be God's love; its building blocks are what the Holy Spirit puts on your heart to share or do, and the mortar is the intense faith that God is going to do a great work with whatever time we spend, whether we hit immediate pay dirt or not. Transformation and patience go hand in hand.

The core of engaging in the process of change is identifying the person's actions and opening up dialogue to draw out the full impact of these behaviors. The person needs to discover how these choices are affecting their life, relationships, and progress. It's only when they own the full ramifications of their actions that we may be used to help redirect the flow of behavior in a godly direction.

Next we help them consider new ways of being. Don't tell them what to do; let them identify that so they can own those steps as well. To ensure that actionable items don't fall flat, inquire about what level of accountability would be best to support them in what they said they would do.

Lastly, encourage them along the way, stay in the game with them, and see it through. The world doesn't need another episode of a Christian not following through on something simply because they were busy, or things got difficult and/or burdensome. What the world needs are Christians who show up, keep up, and live up to what God has commanded: to stand in the gap of despair for those around us. *Spend some time thinking about who you might help today.*

The Question: Who in my life is heading for a fall? Will I step in and trust that God will honor my efforts, or will I pretend the crisis doesn't exist?

33. Responsible Conversations

> Gossip is a one-way dead-end street with stop signs every foot in mouth or so.

Let no corrupt word proceed out of your mouth, but what is good for necessary edification, that it may impart grace to the hearers.

Ephesians 4:29 NKJV

When we think of gossip, we tend to think of it as a practice that divides relationships, when in fact it does something much worse; it weakens the fabric of our own spirit and reduces our influence. It can take the solidity of a person and hollow them into an empty human whose only attentive audience are those equally hollow. Gossipers are conspirators who find enjoyment in belittling others while they ignore the mirror that shows their own condition. *Not a pretty reflection.*

Those who belittle others do nothing
more than belittle themselves.

The common definition of *gossip* is spreading rumors or opinions of someone's personal affairs, usually without their knowledge or all the facts. Sounds almost innocent. As a Christian, though, gossip takes on a whole new meaning, one that if fully understood would convince us to never speak ill of someone again. In the Christian sense, gossip is

1. Speaking about someone with the hopelessness, pessimism, and indifference Satan thrives on;
2. Sharing about another without any spiritual discernment of what God is doing in their life and how he will be glorified through whatever is going on;
3. Proclaiming another's failure for the sake of edifying one's own perceived position or success;
4. An arrogant denial of our own sin nature and living in a ridiculous sense of self-righteousness;
5. A poor witness no matter how artful and clandestine we think we are when doing it; and
6. A direct slam on God's workmanship.

Bottom line? When we gossip, it accurately reflects our own spiritual status. It says something about us that is much more despicable than anything we could say of another and is a poison in circumstances and relationships.

God offers a very clear and workable solution that precedes any form of gossip. When we have a problem or issue with another, we should prepare our hearts and our minds through prayer and meditation and go to that person first before we utter a word to anyone else. If by chance you do speak to someone prior to going to that person, it should be for the sole purpose of getting counsel on how best to steward that interaction. Seeking counsel at this level is not gossip, it is being wise; when done responsibly, it can actually change our heart and bring insight to the circumstance before it gets addressed. It shows a great deal of grace when we avoid slander and speak about others responsibly, and it's an inspiration for others to do the same. So the next time a temptation to instigate or participate in gossip hits you, take the high road and *avoid the one-way dead-end street.*

The Question: In what ways have I gossiped about others lately, and will I have the courage to go to them and ask forgiveness, or at least stop?

34. The Value of Confessing to Others

> Confession is the beginning of the
> breakthrough and end of the stronghold.

Whoever conceals their sins does not prosper,
    but the one who confesses and renounces them finds mercy.

Proverbs 28:13

There is a rarely used, miraculous power in sharing our sin life (confession) with trusted others. It clears the way for lasting transformation unlike any other practice and has the potential to bring healing in a matter of seconds. Unfortunately, we live in a world where maintaining our image or reputation can strangely become more important than the healing that could take place in moments of transparency.

This healing, by the way, can improve our standing with others far more than hiding our sin ever could. If our sins are ongoing, maintaining a front that pretends we're not struggling does nothing more than prevent the inherent beauty and freedom that comes from being honest as it relates to our breakdowns—breakdowns that others understand and can relate to. The payoff for concealment just isn't there, which makes the only real outcomes of not sharing become shame, fear, isolation, and relational awkwardness. Hiding separates instead of unites, and where light shines through transparency, light reduces in power when we become opaque with our sin life.

> Vulner*ability*: the process of giving others the gift
> of truth so they can give us theirs in response.

If we are practicing recurring sin, a common strategy is to cover it up and repeatedly pray to God with no serious intention of dealing with it until we get caught, or the sin creates so much wreckage in our lives that we have to go public and account for it. This is reactive restoration, and the probability for certain bondages to last a lifetime with this approach nears inevitable. Alternatively, proactive restoration, a planned act of confession, assures the best chance of success for killing these strongholds that rob us of the life God desires us to live. I use the words "killing these strongholds," because I wouldn't want you bringing a knife to a gunfight. It's serious business.

As I shared in an earlier point, for many, the idea of confessing sins to one another is an unsettling experience—ironically, more unsettling than living a life in bondage to the sins we're in. But it shouldn't be that way. Once our process of confession to others begins, it will bring light to the fact that we ALL contend with sin—different versions and levels of it, some with deep shame attached and others we've packaged so neatly we barely recognize them as destructive, let alone sinful. Regardless, we will discover that confessing our sin to mature believers, no matter how dark the sin is, will bring a new depth of relationship, while our so-called image actually gets enhanced, not harmed. It's really a form of math: the more confessional conversations you have with "trusted" others and/or counselors, the more perspective you will gain, the less attractive the sin will be, and the looser the stronghold of sin will become until it becomes nothing at all. *Consider the liberty of being set free from recurring sin today.*

The Question: Do I believe that my confession will have others thinking less of me? Or by confessing, will I begin the process of healing, be an example for others to be truthful, and create the space for God to work in mutual truth?

35. Experiencing Consistent Love

> When you view love as a feeling,
> you'll feel love less often.

A new command I give you: Love one another. As I have loved you, so you must love one another.

John 13:34

God places great emphasis on love. He makes it clear that love is the driving force that makes all our natural and spiritual assets effective. Candidly, our gifts and abilities driven without love *are generally useless, unfulfilling, and even destructive.* But there are these pesky things that comingle with love called *feelings*; feelings that often determine whether we are truly loving while doing the things we do. The bad part about feelings is they can become command central for our love, and this reveals itself when *how we feel* determines whether we deliver on our commitments and promises to love others.

I'm sure at this point in life you've noticed that your feelings are unpredictable, often unruly, and sometimes confusing. But what if love wasn't something we feel as much as it is *someone we are,* revealed by the things we do or don't do. And what if the assurance of our experiencing consistent love in our lives was directly related to our commitment to love others *whether we "felt like it" or not*? The answer: we'd *experience* love in its purest, most rewarding form . . . *consistently and beautifully.*

> Love is not a feeling. Love is a commitment
> to serve others with ongoing excellence. The
> feelings, of course, are found therein.

In its most concentrated form, love is a continuum of "in the moment" decisions we make to create value and bless those around us despite how we feel. It springs from the awareness that *we* are the opportunity for love through our commitment to identify the needs, wants, and dreams of others and to confer with God on how to best support others in those things. It is in quiet moments of prayer and reflection that the clarity and creativity to love others in ways that are meaningful and appropriate reveal themselves. Why would God tell us the foundation of all things is love and not collaborate with us in doing so supernaturally? *He wouldn't.*

There's a deep well of extraordinary ways to love if we are willing to contemplate and get creative. If that seems like an abstract process, it can be as simple as asking those you've committed to love for the specific ways they would like to be loved: listen, deliver, repeat, and reap the outcomes from that. Consistency in expressing love removes the appearance of a temporary manipulation and shows others we are committed beyond our feelings—that our love for them has become "front of mind," and that it is important to us: that *they* are important to us. *Love despite how you feel and see how it feels today!*

The Question: Have I considered that if I want to have more love in my life, it will be through the sowing of love that I reap it?

36. Realizing Your Calling

> Our calling is often found in the most unexpected of places—love.

For just as each of us has one body with many members, and these members do not all have the same function, so in Christ we, though many, form one body, and each member belongs to all the others.

Romans 12:4–5

As an advisor, I've been exposed to hundreds of people with varying issues from the basic to the catastrophic. One of the rarer issues brought to me is the question of purpose or calling. Questions like, What is my calling? Why don't I have it yet? How do I get it? When is it coming? are more often thought than voiced. Regardless, before answering these life-altering questions, it's prudent to answer *this one*: What are the two core things God commands us to do in life? (1) Love God with all our heart, mind, soul, and strength; and (2) Love our neighbors as ourselves. As for our callings, they typically become apparent when we're in a healthy degree of obedience to these two basic mandates. God wants us to know that when his two commandments are alive and well in our lives, then our goals, dreams, and visions will have a solid foundation to build upon and the mystery of many things (including one's calling) will often be identified and clarified.

Calling is not a destination. It is an ongoing process that knows no end, only new beginnings. If measured by words, it is the acceptance of one's ability, the understanding of one's unique existence, and the development of one's purpose.

Beyond that perspective of calling and the inherent mystery, what if your true calling was simply *that which you loved to do*? Too good to be true? Unfortunately, there's a flaw that can occur in the Christian mindset that callings should be categorized to a church or ministry need and that there is limited or no availability of calling in doing what we love, especially if it doesn't fit the ministry stereotype. But what if while doing what you loved to do you could fulfill God's two commandments? And what if you could use what you love doing to glorify God, impact others, and be a consistent example of his love? Would that be a calling worth having? One thing is certain: carrying out God's commandments while doing what you love is enjoyable, sustainable, and an incredible . . . *calling*. For example, a friend who loves soccer founded a soccer ministry, another friend who loves sales and marketing mentors business people, while another friend who loves finances learned Dave Ramsey's system and he and his wife impact lives and minister to others that way. They believe in their hearts that this is their calling, and since they love doing it, they don't get tired of it, so they have the energy to improve their gift—making it even more enjoyable and valuable for others.

We're all great at something, and if not, that's a sign of another issue—perhaps disbelief, resignation, or something else. Regardless, most have a skill, ability, gift, or talent to share with others, and sometimes creating the space to use that gift can make way for a calling to come alive. It may take work, but once worked out, it *will* work well and work over time. *Put the gift you are or the talents you have into play today and see if a calling is revealed.*

The Question: If there's currently no place to use my gifting in my life, will I have the courage, tenacity, and discipline to create that space?

37. Understanding Your Enemies

> Are they an enemy of mine . . . or just a sign of the enemy *working in me*?

> The heart is deceitful above all things
> and beyond cure.
> Who can understand it?
>
> Jeremiah 17:9

We all know what a mirror is. Although it reflects a physical image, I always thought a mirror would be more valuable if it reflected a vivid view of our blind spots and the breakdowns waiting to happen that are stored in our character—or perhaps, lack thereof. Painful to think about, I know. One of those areas of breakdown is how we handle those we regard as enemies: those who betray, offend, or simply annoy us in some way. At times, we hold them in a place of contempt in our hearts, unable to connect, relate, or heal; this causes us to avoid them by keeping an emotional or physical distance when the real distance resides inside of us, having nothing to do with them (or geography, for that matter).

> Enemies that show up in life are nothing more
> than an opportunity to build our emotional
> resilience and practice extraordinary love.

But spiritually, this goes much deeper. Not loving our enemies is a sign of Satan working in us. It is also an indication that our current intimacy with God may be a bit of a mirage, as we are missing his strength and compassion to love *ALL OTHERS* unconditionally, creatively, and brilliantly, the way he told us to. Whatever vacancy is left due to the absence of the fruit of the Spirit will be filled with relational instability, inconsistent intimacy, and stagnant growth. We will end up seeing enemies through our own perspective, comfort, and selfishness. The result is that their offense, betrayal, or something as trite as what they said or how they look ends up looking as ugly as the disdain, self-righteousness, and spiritual immaturities that haven't yet been rooted out of us. And then we seem perplexed when people around us don't respond to our filtered attempts at love or involvement in their life, and our bitterness toward them only deepens.

When we are truly loving God with ALL our heart, mind, soul, and strength, our capacity to love others regardless of where they may be or what they may have done rises to a level where emotions and judgments take a backseat to grace and people become something different than what they currently are. We see them through God's eyes, and they become nothing more than an opportunity to show the love of Christ regardless of how they act toward us or what they've done. It is when we live in this rich place of caring in strength that we'll be able to look at those who come against us and ask ourselves, "What is this agitation trying to tell me about myself? How is their offense a provision for my spiritual growth, and how can I love them more intently?" Therein lies the answer to subverting the enemy working within to create a love you'll rarely be without. *See any enemies you think you have from the inside out today.*

The Question: Have I considered that perhaps those I encounter in life and hold as enemies are an indication of my need for spiritual maturing?

38. The Bigness of Little Things

> Our heart and our character are revealed
> in how we handle the details.

His master replied, "Well done, good and faithful servant!
You have been faithful with a few things; I will put you
in charge of many things. Come and share your master's
happiness!"

Matthew 25:23

One of the responsibilities I've carried as a large branding agency
CEO is making sure that I brought the right people into the company so the mission and vision of the organization could be fulfilled and the culture of excellence could be sustained. It was an
ongoing responsibility, but it was critical if we wanted to have
a business that glorified God, represented our values, and delivered our services with excellence to our clients, employees, and
stakeholders. One of the areas we paid close attention to when
bringing people on board was how they handled the details in
their résumé, their presentation of themselves, and small things
like a handshake or the way they engaged with our employees on

a tour. And, of course, how they followed up with us. We were pretty *particular* in our evaluation of new hires and just as diligent in the evaluation of employees who were vying for promotions and raises. The small things mattered. God treats promotion in life no differently.

> Every small decision, every little action, every little step isn't so much about what it gets you; the value is found in the character, confidence, and excellence it builds into you.

It doesn't take much thought to determine whether God has promoted us to rule over much, let alone promoted us at all. A snapshot of our life will be the indicator of that. Are there new forms of oversight, influence, leadership, expansion, and growth driving you into new opportunity, responsibility, territory, and/or even deeper into relationship with others? These are the indicators.

Promotion in life comes when God sees "evidence" in things like keeping a healthy balance of family, career, and ministry—caring for the people and initiatives in both the big things and the small things, the few and the many things. But as ruler over our lives, God desires to put us in places where we belong and in situations we can handle. So when he sees a casual commitment in handling the small or the few basic things that we often take for granted, overlook, or fail to follow through on, God's promotion *may* stop until the development of our character reaches a place that is promotable—a place where we care about the details and how they affect lives and initiatives. One thing is certain: God desires that we grow into positions of greater influence and reach, but he desires us to handle those new positions of influence with Christlike love and execution . . . *and in that,* he is glorified. *Consider whether the character you are exemplifying is promotable, both in the natural and the spiritual sense today.*

The Question: Are there positions or roles I'd like to be in that may be stalled because my execution isn't aligned to withstand the demands of the new position?

39. Getting Closer to Our Parents

> After we turn eighteen, if we want
> to get closer to our parents, it's up
> to us to make that happen.

And over all these virtues put on love, which binds them all together in perfect unity.

Colossians 3:14

There comes a time in life when our parents' job is finished (for the most part). At that point, they have a life to live, retirement to prepare for, and old age to contend with—some of which would make raising kids seem like child's play.

For many children, real intimacy and love from their parent(s) were missing during their upbringing and still are today. But again, if you're over eighteen, your parents' job is complete; good or bad, you've been raised, and *trust me*, they are moving on to new things. There comes a time in every child's life where it will be opportune to accept that any great rewards or new growth in relationship with our parents will come from how *we* sow into it, meaning if we want to have something different than what we currently have, it will come from *us to them* and not from them to us.

It would be even wiser to remove any leftover expectations that this or that will change and somehow our parents will start delivering some of the things we missed in our upbringing or that are currently missing in the relationship. They simply may not know how, or perhaps the roots of their relational shortcomings may be too deep to pull out. Some roots grow deeper over time.

> It's amazing how much my parents have
> changed since I've changed.

Of course, our own roots can grow deep over time, and things like bitterness, resentment, and unforgiveness can linger; at that point all our attempts to love will be corrupted by those attachments, and the fruit of our attempts will be spoiled or rotten. Notable and positive change requires a mature moment of saying, "Up until now it's been one way with my parents; from now on I'm going to bring something new to the relationship, without reserve or expectations, but with a full commitment regardless of how I feel or what I think I deserve." The transformation will happen by sowing differently, loving unconditionally, dropping our agendas, and engaging with what is important to them *for a change.* It requires a form of self-sacrifice that resembles many of the same sacrifices our parents made while raising us—the sacrifices we conveniently forget about regardless of how well we thought they did. Better relationships with our parents (and with others) will generally come from us to them and rarely the other way around. *Embrace the idea that if things are going to be different, it's up to you to be different today.*

The Question: What can I do and who can I be to bring greater fulfillment to my relationship with my parents, siblings, or other relatives?

PS: I did this with my father many years before he passed. One day, I reached out to him and asked if we could meet halfway for lunch; we did this many times. Turns out these were the most rewarding, memorable conversations of my life with my father, and now that he is gone, I am thankful that we had this time. I'm grateful I reached out—not quite knowing what the outcome would be, but knowing I could love him and appreciate him for who he was and perhaps get to know him better . . . *and I did*. We left nothing off the table, and these are the conversations I cherish most.

40. How Stillness Accelerates Progress

> If you want to accelerate your Christian maturity, stay perfectly still.

Consider how the wild flowers grow. They do not labor or spin. Yet I tell you, not even Solomon in all his splendor was dressed like one of these. If that is how God clothes the grass of the field, which is here today, and tomorrow is thrown into the fire, how much more will he clothe you—you of little faith!

Luke 12:27–28

Have you noticed the pace of life lately? Perhaps you've been moving so quickly, you've had little time to think on it. Or perhaps you have become so accustomed to being carried in life's stream of busyness that it just seems normal—until one day, in a moment of "too fast, too much, too often" you cry out, "Stop the world, I have to get off." Perhaps you get a flash of reprieve only to land back in the stream near the same pace as before. And who suffers for this unfounded, unwarranted, even unproductive pace? We do, by missing the wisdom, insights, and perspective we will find in moments of stillness. There are also those around us who pay a price for our pace, as even when we're in their midst our attention is distracted and the presence of "I've got something to do, I've got someplace to be" brings the potential of the relationship to a quick halt.

Slow down; good things happen there.

It's ironic that we start out life waiting in one place for about nine months only to be in a frenetic hurry for the rest of our lives. We think that by moving faster, thinking faster, and acting faster, things will happen faster and better. *For the most part and in the long run, they won't.*

Slow is the new fast, calm is the new force, and peace is the new progress for those who are intent on making things happen and are committed to the work ethic to do so. In contrast to the world's view, stillness in God's economy doesn't mean stuckness; it means progress and access to a whole new set of tools for all of life. To live from a place of stillness (even when we're operating in urgency) means that slowing down and tapping into God's thoughts, strength, and wisdom in real time will create greater efficiencies while improving outcomes across the board of our life. I call it "Stillumination": our perspective and vision are brought into God's light where things are seen clearly, without obstruction of self or external noise. It's like getting a perpetual provision of life signs and direction. Ultimately, we avoid recklessness and crashes in life and get to our destinations quicker with less stress if we're in touch with the Direction Giver.

The commitment to be at rest for a moment and engage with God in stillness can occur at any time and any place. As I shared before, after a bit of practice, it takes but a moment to get to that amazing, peaceful spot where God's directions are sound and his voice is clear—a minute or three to save hours, days, months, and years of attempting to go it alone in our own strength, without the signs. *Discover the value in moments of stillness while you move through the day today.*

The Question: Am I moving so fast that I am missing the ongoing communication and promptings of the Holy Spirit?

41. The Decision to Doubt

*Sin*icism.

> If any of you lacks wisdom, you should ask God, who gives generously to all without finding fault, and it will be given to you. But when you ask, you must believe and not doubt, because the one who doubts is like a wave of the sea, blown and tossed by the wind.
>
> James 1:5–6

If the truth is that thought precedes ALL action, then where does sin originate? Aside from our good pal Adam, its origins begin in our thought life. However, there is one particular thought-based sin that keeps you from the fullness of the Christian experience, and it probably wouldn't show up as the first answer of the Top 5 Sins survey. Among the most spiritually incapacitating sins is the one we hide deep in the attic of our minds and do our best to conceal from others; the silent sin—the debilitating sin—is fear in the form of *doubt*. Strangely, there's little that's silent about the sin of doubt; we can't hide it from ourselves or God, and (just to be clear) it is as visible to others as is wearing a tuxedo to the gym.

Doubt, as innocent as it seems, makes way for unproductive beliefs to slowly trickle into our minds and eventually lock limitation into our lives. But it is not doubt itself that keeps us captive to a life devoid of adventure and operating in our potential. It is the way we hold on to doubt that is the problem. Rather than accept that we choose doubt over faith, we remain victim to doubt as if it's something that's happened to us, not something that stems from our decision. We blame experiences and external forces for the doubt we choose so there is no one to hold responsible for the thing that brings growth and progress to a dead stop or a slow drip.

Although the prison of our mind has no lock, walls, or fences, we are held captive by the constraint of our beliefs.

Knowing we decide to doubt just like we decide to have faith, we must realize we choose doubt because we derive value from choosing it—*otherwise we wouldn't do it.* The acceptance of this accountable position is the beginning of one's growth and a more predictable development of one's future. So a great question to ask when we doubt something is, "If I was using doubt as a strategy for something, what would it be a strategy for?" Doubt is a strategy we can use to negate responsibility, stay complacent, avoid risk, keep us in our comfort zone, and a dozen other things that keep us *playing not to lose in life* instead of *playing to win.* We choose doubt, which leads us to a stuck life to avoid things like others seeing us fail or adding another black mark on the record of our performance. Yet people love when we risk; they respect it greatly—*sink or swim.*

Bottom line? Choose faith and step in; you'll find everything is good in there—including more engagement with God and others. And when you choose faith over fear, the presence you carry reflects that faith is front-of-mind, keeping you several steps in front of doubt. *Choose faith and watch doubt trail far behind your confidence today.*

The Question: Have I considered that if I want to have more adventure in my life it will come through stepping in and trusting instead of sitting back and rusting?

42. Opportunities Will Pass!

> Taking ownership of our actions is where stagnancy ends and progress begins.

Instead, speaking the truth in love, we will grow to become in every respect the mature body of him who is the head, that is, Christ.

Ephesians 4:15

I sat with a man not too long ago as he complained in great detail about another person. I listened perhaps longer than I should have, and after the rant almost ran out of steam, I asked him, "Yeah, we've all got our brand of messed-up. What's yours?" He was stunned for the moment, but thinking he was justified in his verbal assault, he hit my obstacle like a small speed bump with a *yeah, but* and continued with a destructive whirlwind of rhetoric. After I'd heard enough to identify the dysfunction, I stopped him abruptly, encouraged him to go to the person he had issue with first, voice his concerns, and then get back to me with the outcome. Unfortunately for him, though, rather than take the opportunity to get real about his own contribution to the problem and perhaps use the conversation for something more meaningful, he avoided the reality that anything was wrong with him—you know, things like bitterness, judgment, or gossip, for starters. In this instance it was his loss, as time and opportunity passed. That's the black-and-white nature of our interactions: we either capture and leverage counsel or sabotage and waste it by wanting to vent, gripe, and make excuses.

It's nothing new that sin, bondages, addictions, and character breakdowns are part of our Christian walk. Some of these are circumstantial, some perpetual, and others so subtle they manifest in the tones of our thoughts and actions. Regardless of frequency or power, they keep us from thriving, growing, loving, caring, and many other amazing blessings God has for us.

> A great conversation is one where authenticity
> shows up. Aside from that, there is generally
> manipulation and cover-up.

But there is hope. At the core of any one of our character breakdowns or life challenges, there is amazing value to be found in admitting our role and responsibility. Getting vulnerable, or what I call *rawthentic*, and sharing what is real, what we fear, and how we fall short with God and others can be a terrifying experience if we're not accustomed to it. But while doing so, our eyes become open to what is possible and we see clearly that we can trust God and selected others with the depths of our truth no matter how idiotic it makes us look or how uncomfortable it might be.

It's imperative for Christians to realize that core honesty must be practiced in all life issues in order for catharsis, healing, and character transformation to occur. Without our own reality brought to the surface of our conversations, there is only concealment, pretense, and rearrangement of despair. When you choose to be transparent, you make room for God to accelerate his great works of transformation. The long-term pain of allowing strongholds to govern the important aspects of our life and keep us from experiencing the fullness of God makes the short-term pain of real transparency seem like nothing. *Consider reaching for a new level of transparency in a particular area of your life today.*

The Question: Have I considered the value of sharing my breakdowns with a trusted few to see what God can do in the confines of authenticity?

43. Leveraging Our Most Valuable Asset—Time

> Time is the natural currency of life.
> Do we waste it, spend it, or invest it?

Be very careful, then, how you live—not as unwise but as wise, making the most of every opportunity, because the days are evil. Therefore do not be foolish, but understand what the Lord's will is.

Ephesians 5:15–17

Depending on your age, I can only guess you're like most, saying things like, "Where'd the year go? It's Christmas already, and wow—time flies." Time and life are moving at a rapid rate, yet in a day we all get the same 1,440 minutes—never more, never less. Because most get a fair amount of years on the planet, we rarely break out the stopwatch to evaluate how we steward those minutes and the urgent or casual way in which we hold them. And yet time is accountable to 1,440 minutes a day; that which is lost (or wasted) may never be regained.

When we think of stewardship, money is usually the first thing that comes to mind. But time transcends money. Time cannot come from money, but money can be acquired from time. Time is the foundation of all things, and its worth is incomparable, yet few sermons and little thought go into stewardship of time and the urgency therein. Perhaps it is because we tend to view our lives in months and years rather than hours, moments, and seconds. The problem with a long-sighted, casual view of time is that it numbs any sense of urgency about life and what is possible in our time here. It creates the illusion that there is an endless supply of time, and it spurs procrastination and a way-too-casual attitude toward the gift of life. As a result, we default to "I'll get to it later," or "I'll do it someday."

> We often look forward to what our time will bring, but it's better to look at what we will bring to our time.

If we want to be wise as a serpent over our most precious asset, we must eliminate our vague interpretations of life and leverage the value of our time in hours, minutes, even seconds—NOT white-wash it into a seemingly endless number of years. Although it's not about counting our minutes, *it is* about making our minutes count and being intentional with God's gift of time. We must be deliberate as we plan each day and give credence to what God wants to do in every moment, situation, and conversation. Sometimes it's a great idea to look at the approximate time you have left on the planet and design the macro visions you have and things you want to achieve from the end of your life backward. This gives a sobering vantage point of time, helping us discover what is possible with the approximate time we have left and revealing what must be done in increments to have our visions become reality.

In its most distilled form, stewardship of our time shows reverence for the life we've been given—so much so that we take it with seriousness so we can experience more of its true value. When we learn to value each moment, real fulfillment shows up. It's something like "gratefulness of time" creates "great fullness *in time.*" *Consider your time as the precious gift it is today.*

The Question: Do I look at time with little urgency and live on earth as if there is an endless supply? *There isn't—not on earth anyway.*

44. Praying Comprehensively

> Whenever you pray for something—a situation, challenge, or crisis—don't forget to pray for the way you are relating to what you are praying for.

And when you pray, do not keep on babbling like pagans, for they think they will be heard because of their many words.

Matthew 6:7

When I sat down with a young man one morning, he began to open up about a particular crisis. He shared the problem, the details, and the impact—and although I began to connect him to what God had to say about crisis, he bounced right back to sharing about the crisis. It's not uncommon for one to want to hang out with a problem and vent over it many different ways with many different people, but this is not the path to gain strength. In fact, it is an all-but-certain way of remaining in the vacuum of the crisis, where each word shared about it reinforces a position that eludes hope and responsible engagement. In short, it is a waste of conversational currency that could be invested instead.

Argue for a limitation on what is possible and
possibility will have reached its limits.

In light of a much-needed redirect (for my sanity and his), I asked him if he had been praying about the problem. Surprised at such an elementary question, he told me he had been praying incessantly about it. He went on to share his disappointment that his prayer had not been answered and believed he could not move ahead or be happy in life unless the problem were behind him. I responded with, "Well, argue for limitation and watch how far it doesn't get you." I paused for a minute to let that sink in, then asked if he'd been praying for the way he is relating to the problem, specifically and with detail. He said he hadn't given it any thought, so I asked if he'd consider that the reason the problem gripped him with such despair might be because he hadn't prayed to have a healthy, godly perspective on what was happening.

I went on to share that it's never the issues in life but how we connect to the issues that determines whether we have victory over them or not. Problems pass: *they always do*. So the victory isn't actually in the thing getting dealt with or getting it behind us; that's simply the clock ticking long enough for the problem to be resolved, lose potency, or be replaced by another problem. Lasting victory comes from the way we display the fruit of the Spirit while spending time in the desert or amidst a trial. At one point in the conversation, I asked him if the problem was designed specifically for him and was an opportunity for him to learn and grow. If it stemmed from something that's not working in his life, what would it be a provision to root out? If you've read this book sequentially, then you've read this question in previous points, because it's one of life's most rarely used but most valuable questions. Everything is a provision.

Every day we pray for the challenges in our life, but an often-overlooked appeal is to ask God to help us relate to what we're praying for so it aligns perfectly with his Word and his promises. Praying in this way is a bold step to renewing our minds so we view problems as valuable, for the edification of our growth, prosperity, and capacity to serve others. *Pray for who you will be in the challenge today.*

The Question: Is my prayer life focused only on getting past the problem or is it equipping me to have victory in the midst of the problem?

45. Sin Loses Its Power

> Don't let the enemy win; serve through your sin.

So I say, walk by the Spirit, and you will not gratify the desires of the flesh. For the flesh desires what is contrary to the Spirit, and the Spirit what is contrary to the flesh. They are in conflict with each other, so that you are not to do whatever you want. But if you are led by the Spirit, you are not under the law.

Galatians 5:16–18

There is brilliance in every believer. It could be based in our expertise, natural abilities, learned skills, experiences, or even our passions. News flash: there are others in life who would love to access that knowledge, so there are infinite opportunities to serve with what we know. Although it's an unfounded and distorted truth, one of the main reasons Christians sit on the bleachers of servanthood is a belief that they are not spiritually healthy enough to engage in instilling themselves and their life experience into the lives of others. It's a twisted view and sometimes an excuse, but most often a tragedy when Satan wins that battle of the mind, neutralizing the potential that exists in how we can each serve others.

News flash two: Last time I checked, Adam's sinful nature is still standard equipment on every human And yet, if there was one recurring truth that keeps Christians on the sidelines of life with their gifts, it would be the statement, "Well, I can't serve God or others because I have sin in my life; I don't 'feel' worthy enough." Shame, guilt, and an ungodly self-image are the potential by-products of sinning that can drive us deep into service resignation. Satan uses how we view and feel about our sin to keep our gifts, abilities, and talents from thriving in the freedom God desires.

> If we are breathing, we are sinning, but never allow this to stop you from being the brilliant person God made you to be and using the brilliant gifts you have.

The idea of fixing ourselves to some self-defined degree before we can step out and serve in our gifts is futile, not to mention a blatant disregard for Christ's redeeming work on the cross. Søren Kierkegaard put it well: "If you are ashamed of your own imperfections, then cast your eyes down before God, not man. Better yet, in weakness decide and go forth!"[1] The decision to exercise our serve despite our sin nature or current or past "sin load" should be made for a number of reasons. First is that the world is in desperate need of experiencing the fullness of our gifts. Second is that God wants to do miraculous things with us and others in the process of serving him. Third, if this is an issue for you, you'll reach the "sin doesn't have to put serving on hold" conclusion someday . . . so *why not today*? Lastly, engaging in serving will draw you into further obedience. As I've said before, serving in this light has a way of eradicating the sins we entertain, as they lose attraction

1. Charles E. Moore, ed., *Provocations: Spiritual Writings of Kierkegaard* (Walden, NY: Plough Publishing House, 2014), 8.

by comparison to the value in using our gifts. *Serve despite your sinful status today.*

The Question: Am I allowing the circumstantial or chronic sin in my life to keep me from serving God? If I served through the sin and experienced the blessing of that, might that move me further from sin?

46. Living a Resolute Christian Life

> It's time to replace some question marks
> in life with some *exclamation points.*

Therefore, my dear brothers and sisters, stand firm. Let nothing move you. Always give yourselves fully to the work of the Lord, because you know that your labor in the Lord is not in vain.

1 Corinthians 15:58

Imagine two piles. One is filled with the things you are uncertain about, the other pile filled with the 100-percent-certain absolutes of your life. Which pile is bigger? It's worth a look now and then. As Christians, we are not destined to go through our days in an unresolved, unsettled state. Life as a believer is not meant to be an uncertain journey filled with doubts about what is true. We've been given God's Word, the Holy Spirit, and a direct channel to God—and yet, if we stare at those two piles, we may be asking ourselves why we have so many question marks and why they are so relentless in destabilizing our journey.

Is God's Word the beginning of the end
of all life's confusion and uncertainty?
No question about it.

A big part of our life consists of old, current, and future questions. Filled with unknowns, uncertainty, and a bunch of other "uns," life seems to get more complex the older we get. I thought the opposite would be true, but I'm beginning to *question* that.☺ Narrowed down to a simplistic form, day-to-day living as well as our growth as believers is a process of turning the question marks of life into exclamation points for many reasons. One of these is to grow into new levels of conviction about our faith. Another is to learn more efficient, effective, and confident ways to deal with the next load of question marks.

I'm sure we'd all like to replace a few current questions with clear answers and have a solid strategy that solves the load of incoming complexities—even a way of dissipating them before they ever hit. The solution? Try connecting every current question mark to a Scripture that brings an exclamation point to it; this is why memorization is so important. It may require our connecting to Scriptures about the various areas of our life in question, but rest assured this will breathe life into our specific circumstances.

Reading just a small bit of God's Word at the start, during, and end of the day has an ability to reduce the quantity of uncertainties we face and turn them into absolutes with amazing speed and consistency. The indwelling of God's Word can make days go by with so much clarity and groundedness that you question nothing, not even yourself. Your disposition becomes so solid that whatever comes your way is answered immediately after it enters your mind and you thrive in God's confidence. The mark of any mature believer is the exclamation mark. *Connect a Scripture to something in question today.*

The Question: Do I have an adequate number of verses in store to contend with the various complexities of my past, current, and future life?

47. The Value of Keeping Our Word

> Every time we break our word we
> put a crack in our character.

All you need to say is simply "Yes" or "No"; anything beyond
this comes from the evil one.

Matthew 5:37

Imagine for a moment if God did not deliver on a commitment that
he made. For example, what if Israel was decimated off the face
of the earth? Or what if any number of biblical prophecies were
to falter or the Word of God proved false in any way? I wonder,
in light of these or other questions like them, what would happen to my belief, my faith, and my resolve for eternal security.
It's evident to me that God *has* delivered on every commitment
he has made thus far in my life, and I believe with the fullness of
my heart that he will continue to do so. That is my faith, and it
is resolute. I hold in the highest regard the importance of God's
Word, his commitment to us, and his covenant. In turn, I must
evaluate my own track record of commitment to God, my wife,

my family and friends, and my business partners. There is much to consider and much to be honest about.

> Raising the bar in keeping commitments will
> lower stress, conflict, confusion, and many
> other things that make life more difficult.

Every day we make commitments; some we view as casual and of minimal importance, while others we hold more seriously. However, to place varying degrees of importance on any of your commitments with others is the beginning of broken relationships, compromised character, and reduced confidence. It adds a bit of abstractness and confusion by adding shades of gray to what is a very black-and-white equation. Our word given, whether casual or serious, made in the past or present, is a contract with ourselves and others that is vital to our mental and spiritual health. Every day you will see some people walking around with a heaviness, only to find out their life is a buildup of broken commitments because they valued how they felt at the moment more than fulfilling their word. What we can't always see is the subversive way that every broken commitment taints our witness and drives us into hopelessness while those around us lose respect, confidence, and trust in our ability to follow through. The result is carrying a weak, hollow presence—one we will never get away from until we begin to keep our word and clean up old, broken agreements with others.

Breaking commitments, agreements, contracts, and covenants is reaching epidemic proportions inside the church and out, breeding distrust, judgment, and bitterness. We can see with our own eyes the grief that broken agreements cast on relationships. And yet there is immediate impact the second we start keeping our word with others. Like turning up a dimmer switch, situations and relationships move progressively from darkness into the light with every promise kept; the future gets brighter with every fulfilled commitment. I promise. *Value others by keeping your word today.*

The Question: Am I keeping all my commitments, large and small? Are there broken commitments out there that I need to fulfill and bring to completion?

48. Listening to Others

> Intentional listening requires faith
> more than it does commitment.

> Nothing should be done because of pride or thinking about
> yourself. Think of other people as more important than
> yourself.
>
> Philippians 2:3 NLV

Ever converse with someone who is mildly to severely distracted? It will probably happen today, and it's one of society's most annoying social practices. Yet despite how many times people are confronted for being distracted, they seem to continue down the road, claiming some excuse for the reason they are not able to focus on what you are saying. And yet, aside from those with severe psychological disorders, if these people were in a life-threatening situation and someone was giving them lifesaving instructions, you can be pretty certain they would grab every word as if, well . . . *their life depended on it*.

In day-to-day living, life doesn't depend on whether you give your undivided attention; relationships and intimacy do, but not life. Regardless of whether my life-threatening example has merit, we listen to others based largely on how much we care to listen and how much we care for those we are listening to.

Bad listeners hear themselves. Average listeners hear the words. Good listeners hear the issues. Great listeners hear the heart.

But why at times don't we listen to those we are in relationship with? Why do we drift off, thinking about other things, while nodding politely, bouncing in and out of the conversation, responding with disconnected responses or sometimes a blank stare? Could be several reasons—selfishness being at the core. The biggest possibility is accepting that in the moment, we are simply lacking in faith.

Let me explain. Whenever we drift, we typically are distracted by thinking about things we think are more important. We think that somehow in the midst of someone talking to us, we are going to discover some value or insight that might impact the important thing we're distracted with. *But there's no time to be effective in that. WE'RE IN A CONVERSATION!* The lack of faith comes in because we don't believe God will honor our giving a full commitment to stay 100-percent focused and pay attention to every word, nuance, body language, etc., so we drift.

Since it's one of my more apparent struggles, I had to ask myself what kind of God I would be trusting if he didn't honor my giving my wife, family, friends, and those who I know or have even just met total focus, knowing he would provide the time necessary to think and deal with ALL other things I might be distracted with. I realized I didn't trust God for that in conversations, so I would dart in and out of them trying to solve the things of my life while in conversations with others. Now imagine talking with Jesus. Do you see him distracted or focused, zeroing in or drifting away?

He's all-in because he values people and he trusts his Father that he can be fully engaged, and all else will be fine.

It honors others when we stay present in conversations, and we gain more enjoyment, insight, and nice surprises when we do so. Say no to distractions and yes to trusting God with the rest of life and whatever other benefit we are deceived into thinking is derived from distraction. *Listen with focus today and see what becomes clear.*

The Question: What could I and others stand to gain if I listened with laser-like focus?

49. The Rhythm of Peace

> There can be a rhythm in our Christianity
> that beats stress into submission.

No discipline seems pleasant at the time, but painful. Later
on, however, it produces a harvest of righteousness and peace
for those who have been trained by it.

Hebrews 12:11

If you lived alone in nature, your mindset would more than likely
move at the pace of the stream, the wind, the snowfall, the sunset,
and the seasons. There's a peace in the metaphor that's undeniable.
But chances are you don't live in nature; you live in a society where
the pace goes from zero to stress just after the alarm clock rings
and before your feet hit the floor. The momentum of the world is
so rapid these days that we mostly move at the speed of anxiety,
and peace becomes collateral damage to the pace. *But there's hope.*

Have you noticed on occasion that your Christian experience
can find a consistently attuned rhythm, a pace where life and relationships are alive, beautiful, and growing with relative ease? We
love that rhythm, and when in it, all things and people seem to be

in the rhythm with us, no matter their missteps or how offbeat *they may be.* It's a neutral place where judgments are minimized, fear loses power, intimacy is maximized, and the enemy can't get in our groove, no matter how slick his moves.

> Changing the trajectory of our life is 101 stuff. Keeping it on course is the real discipline and the real progress.

The rhythm when we are thriving in intimacy with God is a force in motion that can dance through the chaos of life and relationships with the grace of Fred Astaire and the strength of Gene Kelly. Think of a beat you like—for instance, Michael Jackson's "Billy Jean": feel its rhythm, live in it for a few seconds. Now envision the rhythm falling offbeat. Note how you feel as it gets further from where it started into a disjointed cadence that frustrates instead of elevates. Envision the offbeat and how it might affect others, confusing whatever rhythm they may be in because of your unpredictability and chaotic cadence. *Starting to get the picture?* The rhythm here is a spiritual one, tapping into God's pace from the inside out. It's keeping in rhythm with his Word, his strength, and his presence so that the rhythm you move in calms the stresses of life, improves the value of moments, and provides awareness into relationships that would otherwise be missed when you're moving at the speed of disconnectedness.

It's a discipline to stay engaged with God in the momentum of life—living in the Spirit where his rhythm lives . . . keeping the beat in perpetual seconds and minutes, not on sporadic occasions when we desire something from God or become desperate. It's a commitment we make to stay in sync with the flow of God's pace; we stay in the disciplines of seeking, learning, risking, sowing, and loving so we can govern over the pace and trajectory of all things. Due to the demands of life, it's not always easy to stay in the rhythm—but the benefit outweighs the investment, infinity to one. *Stay in the rhythm of the Spirit today; God's there.*

The Question: Are my spiritual habits in need of some tuning? What would life be like if I could always be in rhythm with God's presence?

50. More Predictable Change

Change is choice, not chance.

But grow in the grace and knowledge of our Lord and Savior Jesus Christ. To him be glory both now and forever! Amen.

2 Peter 3:18

Although change is hard and we may not always like the idea of it, change for the better in many areas is a desire for most Christians. Perhaps the idea of change is attractive because we are called to be in a continual state of spiritual transformation, and today there is great need for us to be moving to a new place of maturity, capacity, and influence as believers (all good things). Regardless, we have a love/hate relationship with change.

The equity of our time will always be enhanced
by the quality of our discipline.

The main rub with change (getting to a new place where we are better off than before) is we're not always welcoming of the work that ensures it. In fact, rather than invest thought into what transformation will require tangibly, not just mentally, we often waste the same mental currency fantasizing about change instead of strategically planning for it. It's deceptive to think repetitive fantasizing creates motivation, when in fact dreaming about change repetitively tends to demotivate, derail, and in some cases destroy the possibility of change before it even starts. It's a cycle that, if not moved to an actionable process, will bring our belief system to a place where dreams, visions, and goals drift further and further from our confidence into an abyss of stuckness. I know; I've been there.

Based on my own experience and the privilege of counseling others, I've discovered that lasting inspiration and motivation come 5 to 10 percent into the process of engaging in change, rather than at the beginning when just thinking about things. It's experiencing small wins and actual growth that creates the momentum needed to move through obstacles and break down walls that are certain to show up in the process. It is in the action that collaboration with God takes on real meaning and moves to a dynamic, fresh exchange, providing an energy that will sustain motivation. *Thinking alone just doesn't do that.* Even if the challenges of discipline and action reveal our shortcomings, the collaboration with God and continuance of our action will bring about the appropriate change along with ancillary changes—changes that will surprise us beyond whatever we may have originally anticipated. Action adds value everywhere.

Although there are times when God gifts a change of heart, mind, or circumstance, I believe that most of the time he desires to use us to create change, and there is often more value for us in the *process of change* than the actual change itself. The real value is in the journey, the struggle, and the new relationship that is formed with him along the way. The change or achievement we experience is simply a symbolism of that new relationship. *Take some things you've been thinking about and move them into discipline today.*

The Question: What one thing could I stretch myself into where I have a fair assumption I'd be a new person at the end of it?

51. Giving from an Authentic Heart

> Just because you're *giving* doesn't mean you're a giver.

But when you give to the needy, do not let your left hand know what your right hand is doing.

Matthew 6:3

Confession time: there is a percentage of both selfishness and selflessness in all my giving. If I look closely, I'll find some percentage of me looking out for me, not just the recipients of my giving, in every gift, tithe, sowing, ministry, or other giving situation. Sometimes it's minor or almost nonexistent; at other times it's pretty front and center. I would say it's not intentional to soften it a bit, but *it is* intentional because I'm choosing to entertain selfish ambition at some level in the process. It happens *to all of us in varying degrees* during different times of our life.

One thing I've noticed is that when I have a weighted self-interest in giving, the experience of giving loses its richness, its purity. But is it realistic to hit a 100-percent selfless giving disposition? According to the Word and with our strength in Christ, the answer is yes. We have been given that power and much more.

> If we all understood the power in giving over taking, and how little it takes to give, we wouldn't always give in to feeling taken or the need to take. So always take the opportunity to give.

What makes the act of giving a blessing to *us* is that we are in a state of gratefulness while giving and experience the joy in doing so—a healthy blend of humility and appreciation. What also makes giving a blessing to us and to others is that it comes from a genuine, caring heart with no strings attached, no agenda or expectations of acknowledgment, praise, or return; God's got that covered. When our focus is fully others-centered, we are trusting God for our compensation or value in this process. And as we empty ourselves, we allow the empty vessel to be filled with what God knows we need, not what *we* invent that we need. It creates a freedom to give in faith, a release that removes the tainted feel that comes with agenda-based giving that desires something in return. I believe the value behind anonymous giving removes much, if not all, temptation to edify self in the process.

To be conscious that we don't always give out of pure motives should give us hope that we can increase the unconditional nature of our giving, making it more about the other and less about us—the way it should be. *Check your heart in all the ways you give today.*

The Question: Am I growing in the area of giving all gifts to others with no expectations or agendas, or am I hanging on to things I could easily release to the Lord?

52. The Value of Relevant Learning

> Reading with relevance overcomes
> strongholds with dominance.

A wise man is full of strength,
  and a man of knowledge enhances his might.

Proverbs 24:5

Whenever I ask a believer what they're struggling with in life and they share what it is, one of the foundational questions I ask is what they're currently reading. Ironically, 90 percent of the time, the topic they're reading about has nothing to do with their struggles. Instead, it's the latest and greatest book that a friend, relative, or pastor told them to get or sections of the Bible that are unrelated to the struggle. I find this odd, because if I went to the emergency room with a severe head laceration, I wouldn't ask for a pair of crutches. *But that's just me.*

When you embark on a specific learning curve,
specific transformation is just around the corner.

It goes without saying, we all have areas in our lives where we need healing or would like to grow. But rather than prioritize these areas with focus and intentionality, it seems the norm to read or access unrelated content, while the specific learning we need immediately gets pushed off for something more intriguing, or something that may numb the pain of whatever's not currently working in life. Understandable, but not optimal.

For example, some time ago I was sitting with an older man whose marriage was in trouble. I asked him about the severity and he said divorce had been discussed. So after a few moments passed, I asked him what he was reading these days. "End-times prophecy," he said. I replied, "Perhaps at this juncture, you should be more concerned about the end of your marriage than end-times prophecy, just a guess." We both (kinda) laughed, he conceded, and *The 5 Love Languages*, Corinthians, and a marriage intensive program became his learning focus for a while, as did getting some professional help with his wife in couples counseling.

Since we were going to be meeting together in a mentor relationship, I told him the most effective way for him to grow quickly was that we would be dialoguing about material that is very specific to the breakdown. I shared with him that after learning the specifics he needed to know, he would be able to bring them into his marriage and put the principles to use. That would give us something very clear and tangible to discuss using real-life scenarios, not engaging in hypotheticals and recycling baggage. A significant way those in counseling or any form of therapy can accelerate their healing is by bringing more concentration to learning about what is at hand rather than counting on the counselor to wave a magic wand for things to get better. We have to pay a price to grow, but the good news is that a little goes a long way; once we understand the power of *specific learning*, future problems will stand little chance.

Whether it deals with our current inventory of issues or the skeletons in our closet, a journey of focused learning in any area of our life will reap supernatural dividends. I believe when God sees us working diligently on a chosen stronghold, he takes note and adds to the process in ways we don't understand but benefit from. And at the end of the journey when the learning sinks in, transforms our life, and begins to bear fruit, we discover one more way God performs miracles. *Consider what area of your life needs attention and bring some key knowledge to the fight today.*

The Question: Is my reading addressing the areas of my life that need prioritized attention?

53. Our Available Strength

> As believers, our resources are infinite, powerful, and immediate.

The weapons we fight with are not the weapons of the world. On the contrary, they have divine power to demolish strongholds.

2 Corinthians 10:4

I'm not overexaggerating: just about every prayer I hear these days includes someone asking to attain things they already have, or to get to a status they are already at, and to become someone they already are. The tone and manner in many prayers is near that of a plea, not a proclamation. If we listen, we'll hear God say, "I already gave you that, you are equipped, and by the way, as Christ has told you over and over again, you've been *given* the power to do greater things than he." You'll notice *given* is in the past tense, and so it is done, finished, installed, ready for use.

At our time of conversion there were unlimited spiritual assets and attributes permanently woven into the fabric of our heart, mind, soul, and spirit. But most of these assets remain untapped and unused because we fail to recognize they are even there. It's as if at times we believe the attributes given to us are stored in a closet in heaven somewhere, only to be distributed if we're in the right place at the right time with the right heart or whatever we make up about our right to access and use these powerful assets. God wants a different level of understanding for believers, where recognition of our strength, wisdom, and discernment are a belief away, instead of a request away. Think about it—even if you requested a particular trait and it was delivered on a silver platter, you'd still have to believe you have it in order to put it into play, and the effectiveness of the trait would be relative to the level of belief attached to it.

> Is it better to feel a need to chase after strength, confidence, and wisdom, or better to acknowledge we already have them?

So what systemic problem shows up with Christians to de-power them into a state of the constant need for things that they already have before they reach for new goals, try new things, or deal with life's challenges? In many cases it is limiting belief about our inherent spiritual strengths and who we are in him. We must remember we have inherited through Christ in us the opportunity to come into an "I have" mindset relating to all God-given spiritual assets (you know . . . those things we constantly pray for but already are in possession of). Not saying we are God here, but through the acknowledgment of Christ in us, it's the difference between saying, "Lord, give me peace" versus saying, *I have peace*, or "Lord, give me patience" versus proclaiming, *I have patience*, or asking, "Lord, give me joy" instead of acknowledging, *I have joy*. Operating in life with this divine realization will not only equip us to expand our own territory, but we will *have* plenty of resources left to overflow into the lives of others.

When the Lord tells us our weapons *are* mighty (*are*, meaning they exist already) we should consider gaining more awareness of what they are and the potential they will have if we come into complete agreement and maintain a minute-by-minute awareness that we carry them at the ready. *Acknowledge who you are and how you've been equipped today.*

The Question: Have I been living as if I need to get to a place, become someone, or attain something before I can experience great things in my walk?

54. Keeping Intimacy in Marriage

> More than 50 percent of Christian married men struggle with pornography. That ain't the half of it . . .

But each person is tempted when they are dragged away by their own evil desire and enticed. Then, after desire has conceived, it gives birth to sin; and sin, when it is full-grown, gives birth to death.

James 1:14–15

According to Provenmen.org, 55 percent of married men have struggles with pornography,[1] and that might be conservative. As for women, the numbers hover around 20 percent. Statistics vary, but the numbers, however, aren't startling as much as the effects of pornography that end up in marriages. It is a silent killer that rips the spirit of the marriage union to shreds . . . secretly, quietly, click by click by click.

---

1. Provenmen.org. Pornography survey statistics.

Based on my own research and counseling others, from the moment we engage in pornography, our interest in intimacy begins to wane. Our spouses slowly appear less attractive to us and their physical touch becomes at first distant, then awkward to uncomfortable, edgy, and ultimately potentially repulsive. While life is breathed into the pixels of pornography, touch goes away, the sex life dies, and within a short time, our spouses sometimes become nothing more than objects that get in the way of our fantasies and carrying them out. That's the hard truth. Just Google pornography's effect on the brain to learn more.

> Our image of ourselves and our relationship is destroyed as we view the images of pornography.

What's worse than the obvious destruction is that *if* we're on the betrayed end and the addiction is concealed from us, we begin to invent reasons why things have changed. *I am not attractive anymore. Maybe they're seeing someone else. I'm getting old; it's getting old.* We know something's wrong, but we don't know exactly what it is. So the betrayed gets an array of repercussions from the other's addiction without knowing the real truth. The betrayed winds up with no intimacy, feels unattractive and unvalued, and has the added bonus of blaming themselves for the deadness in the marriage.

Whether a person is single or married, an ongoing relationship with pornography brings with it a shame that shows itself in every expression we share, every word we say, and every feeling we have. It's like a toxic syrup poured over our body, mind, and spirit that we carry around in life, and people sense we are in bondage more than we know.

It's ironic that the very tool Satan uses to keep us in deep shame is the same tool that can help get us out of it . . . *the internet.*

to "turtle," as there are many who need help from us. It is, however, a summons to stick your neck out with a compassionate
heart to make a difference. It's a call to speak into the lives of
others with grace and truth and avoid the temptation to engage
in a self-righteous, self-aggrandizing, "I've got it figured out"
manner. *We* don't *have it figured out*; we are all equally figuring
it out relative to our own commitment and where we are on our
journey.

Approaching others in transformational work will always be
more effective and fulfilling with humility and grace present,
regardless of how soft or hard you condemn the issue. I say
"condemn the issue," because condemning the person will cause
defense and resentment, and will shut down the conversation,
where addressing the impact of the issue will open dialogue and
opportunity.

> Not every conversation will change someone's life, but
> then again, any one conversation can . . . and some do.

Many Christians today have become too comfortable dancing
on the surface of conversation in the name of political correctness—exchanging pleasantries while people around them are train-
wrecking—because we don't want to offend anyone and would
rather be liked than risk making a difference. Political correctness
often leads to ignoring what's in front of you, while politeness
steps into it with gentleness and the right heart.

The beauty of gracefully addressing issues, sharing your conviction, and ushering new possibilities into situations is that it
can be viewed as a practice and developed skill while knowing
that it is God who does the work, not us. We can always enter in
with gentleness, kindness, humility, and the support of the Holy

Spirit—logs or no logs. *Take some conversational risks in grace and love today!*

The Question: Who in my life is headed for trouble, and who could stand to be impacted with a conversation of love, truth, and encouragement?

56. Tapping into God's Brilliance

Discernment is the direct link between
God's voice and our spirit.

When a country is rebellious, it has many rulers,
    but a ruler with discernment and knowledge maintains
    order.

Proverbs 28:2

Recount the outcome of a situation where a crystal-clear insight changed everything for you. It's easy to remember, as there was a certainty about you that you probably would like to never go away. There was an acuteness to the circumstances and others that made things less tense and provided a sense of ease. That's *discernment*, and it has the capacity to position you in a place of resourcefulness in just about any situation like few other assets.

Discernment is more of a practice birthed in intentionality than a gift. Unlike prophecy, where one is speaking a word from God, discernment of situations and people leaves room for error. Discernment can be off and on, and its accuracy is largely dependent on our relationship with the Holy Spirit as we engage with life and others, despite our skill level.

The Holy Spirit's voice is like a pure satellite radio station. Call it K-YOU. It is a 100-percent personalized, twenty-four-hour-a-day channel speaking words of clarity, wisdom, and discernment to YOU specifically, perfectly and brilliantly. It never stops speaking; and given you are committed to a frequency of awareness and serious about tuning in, you will glean insights that will improve every aspect of your life and ensure every part of your ministry and difference-making are more effective and enjoyable.

Ministry done in our own strength, without discernment and wisdom, misses most of its potential.

Depending on our distraction level in life, sometimes the signal is gone—no voice, dead silence. Other times it's static-ridden and you hear bits and pieces but nothing clear, lots of white noise. Then there are times the signal is locked—a perfectly clear transmission of God's leading, voice, and peace in full surround sound; it's called walking in the consciousness of God, and our bandwidth for serving in it and the fulfillment we derive from it is nothing short of miraculous. Tuning in to the channel will serve every aspect of our Christianity with a new collaboration; the communication becomes a two-way channel where inquiry for answers and dialogue for guidance elevate to a new level of access and exchange in real time.

Unfortunately, many don't experience the fullness of this divine channel where God delivers amazing discernment for our life and the lives of others. The reason? Our stations are tuned to other channels like K-STRESS, K-SELF, K-STRIVE, K-NUMB, etc. So what is the value of God's perfectly preprogrammed 24/7 K-YOU broadcast? I'll keep it simple and say, "Stay tuned." *Live life with a clear channel of communication today.*

The Question: What will be my new disciplines to stay tuned to the frequency of God's communication?

57. Our Sin Has Value for Others

> The sin we once lived in shouldn't breed regret, it should create opportunity.

But I have prayed for you, Simon, that your faith may not fail. And when you have turned back, strengthen your brothers.

Luke 22:32

Consider the word *sin*. What happens when you hear it? Does the word itself bring a slight sense of tension and a desire to flee from the thought, or is there a more serious feeling of shame, even despair or hopelessness? Perhaps it creates a feeling of conviction over what is going on in our lives right now. These negative feelings are normal if you're simply a human being. Sin, or the thought of it, is not supposed to necessarily drive positive emotions—*but it can*.

Our specific sin, if held in his light, becomes an opportunity to serve from a place few others can.

There is something inherently valuable to be discovered in our sin. Not the continuance of sin, but the opportunity that exists in it, once the sin is dealt with . . . *for good* (pun intended). It's another reveal of God's infinite wisdom and strategic application in bringing beauty to life in us when we miss the mark, using *all things* despite the nature of the breakdown. People who have lived in a particular kind of sin have a rare opportunity to minister from their unique sin experiences like no one else can. In fact, for some who are struggling in sin, the only counsel they'll listen to or respect comes from those who have gone through the actual or similar experiences. It shouldn't be this way, but it mostly is. So rather than hold past sins as a burden of any kind, we can look forward to the opportunities we have and the specific experiences we've had in that area, because in many ways, we are an expert in that category of sin and the healing process to help others.

Ministry will always be derived from the sins we've been healed from and the trials we've been through. The level of groundedness and conviction we possess through our experiences is a force that cannot be discredited or debated; it goes beyond theory, because we lived it in reality.

So if you'd like to consider a new area of ministry, look first to what you've been through and have dealt with. There is an opportunity to make a notable difference there, and no shortage of people struggling with the same issues. *See the brilliance in all things today, even past sin experiences that will be used now or in the near future.*

The Question: What area of breakdown or sin have I overcome that I could help others overcome?

58. Being Future Minded, Not Past Polarized

> Driving through life looking in life's rearview mirror is "know" accident.

Forget the former things;
  do not dwell on the past.
See, I am doing a new thing!
  Now it springs up; do you not perceive it?
I am making a way in the wilderness
  and streams in the wasteland.

Isaiah 43:18–19

By the time we hit *age six*, experts say our past (the whole six years of it) will determine how we live out the rest of our lives. They call these the *formative years*, and it would be wise to note it was not God who said this, but modern psychology. Although there's some truth in this notion, it is far from law and shouldn't be held as such, nor should any other indicator that our past will determine our present and future. That just doesn't exist in God's Word or his promise. Although impactful, all the theories, labels, and treatments of psychology pale in comparison to adopting this one truth: "I am not my past; I am who God says I am." Unfortunately, though, people spend more energy arguing for their psychology than they do proclaiming the truth that God has provided them.

Aside from circumstances beyond control, a hard reality for many Christian adults who are not content with their lives is that most current excuses for why life isn't working are used up. So the only workable one left is that *the past* is the reason why the present and future can't be in their full potential. The weight of whatever once was has conveniently become the justification to avoid bold moves in life, and we give power to "our upbringing"—something that no longer exists. We end up living in the grave of our past, where the only possibility that exists is to let our past die on the altar we place it on . . . *if we choose to.*

The clearer your vision for your future,
the more blurred your past becomes.

It's no surprise that living in the fullness of Christ is not a trouble-free, risk-free zone. It can appear easier and safer at times to use the past as an excuse to avoid new territory because we lose the predictability to look good, feel good, be right, and be in control: all illusions, all insufficient for any lasting gratification and growth. The lie is that there is safety in not risking. Being in risk is the safest place a believer can be, as engagement with God accelerates and creates new standards of confidence because we're in the present, stretching, depending on, and dialoguing with God for ALL our strength, courage, and clarity.

The Christian life calls us to run the race to win. And when we run to win we will fall short and fall down. But we will always fall forward as long as we are looking forward and keeping the past in check. I doubt many victories would be had if we were looking in life's rearview mirror during the race. *Put the past in its place and live from an amazing new spot today.*

The Question: What parts of my past am I holding on to that may be having a limiting effect on future moves?

59. Be Exceptionally You

When it comes to living life as "fully ourselves," take the risk and just *be.*

> I care very little if I am judged by you or by any human court; indeed, I do not even judge myself. My conscience is clear, but that does not make me innocent. It is the Lord who judges me.
>
> 1 Corinthians 4:3–4

For most of my early childhood through my early adulthood, I lived most days in a manufactured disposition, casting out a partially fabricated presence; the end product of "me" was a person others couldn't really connect with or relate to. As such, life was relationally awkward, unpredictable, and at times, *lonely.* For whatever reason, I always felt the need to become a little different than who I actually was in the circumstances, and I'd adjust my words or behavior to make myself appear relevant or important just to fit in. I would think and act in a way that I thought would be perceived as valid without any real awareness that if I was just myself, life would work better in the short and long run.

When we avoid being authentic with others we
become a fugitive from true relationship.

The practice of continually packaging ourselves for the approval of others is in stark contrast to just being fully ourselves and seeing how God honors that strange and unusual concept. The conundrum is, if we don't combat the need to perform, we never get to refine our true selves. We end up buffing and polishing the plastic of our veneers, and although we may think we look more presentable on the outside, the inside is crying out to just be real and be free. And if we drop the façades and just act fully ourselves, we end up in the process of seeing what shows up in our life from that place and refining our *real* self. Not only do we make quicker progress in the long run, we also get to experience the immediate freedom and liberty of just being ourselves and stepping off the stressful stage of life—killing the people-pleasing adjustments once and for all.

It's not often talked about, but it's a major goal of our spiritual journey to be at peace with who we are in Christ. It's not always easy, and there are many reasons we feel the need to pretend. But people pleasing and adjusting our behavior away from who we are is worse than giving the "fullness of ourselves" a try and refining what shows up along the way.

I believe one of the bigger joys of God's heart is when we come into a restful place, content in all our insecurities, shortcomings, and failures, knowing it is Christ who stands in the gap of our weakness and nothing else. It's the practiced admittance of our frailty and weakness in tandem with claiming his strength that creates the freedom to discard all façades and just be ourselves and refine from there. It's when we enter this place of surrender, trust, and proclamation that we truly become clay, ready to be molded into new things for God's great work. *Drop any pretense and live in the freedom to be exactly who God made you to be today.*

The Question: Are there areas of my life where I could drop a little pretense and just be fully myself?

60. Removing Deadweight from Life's Journey

> Each day must be dealt with,
> within the confines of itself.

Therefore do not worry about tomorrow, for tomorrow will worry about itself. Each day has enough trouble of its own.

Matthew 6:34

If the peace and joy in your life weren't measured by how you feel but what others experienced from you, would they register near the same? Or are others looking in, noticing discontentment, restlessness, and other attributes that may have them looking at your status in life as questionable, even undesirable? In other words, are they saying, "I don't see anything different enough to inquire how they acquired what they have"? It's a sobering thought, but candy coating aside, the foundation of our witness of our life in Christ has little to do with what we feel or think or the words we proclaim, but what shows up in our attitudes, actions, and responses to life.

One way to create more peace, joy, and consistency is to acknowledge that life discontentment or restlessness rarely manifest in our lives from a single significant event. They can, of course, but mostly they are the result of a buildup of daily issues, problems, bad behaviors, and bad habits left unresolved, causing them to spill over into the next day and into our mindset until they become engrained in our attitude. If enough time passes, they compound into an insurmountable burden that spurs stress, mild to chronic anxiety, even pervasive anger and depression, which makes sweeping issues under the proverbial carpet quite dangerous. The strategy of dealing with an excessive load of these things once in a while will work, but if we live in postponement and avoidance of daily dealing, we will carry an unnecessary burden, resulting in lower overall life satisfaction and again, a poor witness. The real danger is when we avoid issues for so long that they become more difficult to recognize and deal with.

> A more fulfilled life surfaces as we resolve broken
> relationships and broken commitments and
> handle problematic issues in real time.

In contrast to avoidance as a practice, the habit of dealing with what comes up within the confines of that day gives us opportunities to deal in smaller, more focused bits that aren't mixed into the confusion of other undone stuff. They are in better focus, and our mental and spiritual capacity to manage them is greater and more distinct. The confidence and skills we gain through this discipline can make whatever comes up in the day have us saying, "No big deal" rather than, "I can't deal." The outcome is that we perform better, feel better, sleep better, and are clearly more effective for the kingdom. *Deal with what comes up today, and see how tomorrow provides more in every respect.*

The Question: What messes and undone stuff would be good to consider cleaning up over the next thirty, sixty, or ninety days?

61. Faithing Forward

> Faith is the currency of the Christian.

And we also thank God continually because, when you received the word of God, which you heard from us, you accepted it not as a human word, but as it actually is, the word of God, which is indeed at work in you who believe.

1 Thessalonians 2:13

When I hear of an uber-wealthy individual (Christian or not) who while in a state of stress or depression commits suicide, it twists my mind a bit. The fact that they had unlimited resources to spend to have fun, travel, eat the best foods, have the best cars and homes, give notably to great causes, and get the best help for whatever was in the way of their contentment forges the reality that monetary currency means little in God's economy of fulfillment. No matter how much is in the bank account, money's capacity to buy anything other than temporary comforts is nil. A believer has an account far more valuable than money called *faith*; and yet, like any account, our balance can be healthy or near bankrupt.

Faith is not just knowing what is true
but acting on what you believe.

When we move into a new territory in any area of our life, it's wise to check the balance in our faith account to see what is there for the journey. If the account is near empty, the norm is to operate in our own strength, believing in ourselves to make things happen. Then when things don't work out, our faith account takes another hit, leaving only more skepticism for what's ahead. Faith precedes everything, and when our faith is inconsistent, mediocrity lives, dreams die, and we resign ourselves to a life of complacency that we conveniently call "a normal life."

We know the faith of a mustard seed can do much, meaning our faith is always at some level, but strengthening our faith equity is no different than building financial equity. Pragmatically, we make a commitment toward it and the account grows. Don't put in the work, and our faith equity has a way of compounding backward while shrinking our life to a low-adventure world that resembles a dull shade of beige. This is not the way of the believer, as we will wither inside if we aren't consistently putting our faith into action. But those who *are* willing to step out, live out their vision, create worthwhile goals, and step into their call will always have (for lack of a better phrase) "faith momentum," and if they fail they'll still have a great time doing it. How can one have a great time by failing? Faith covers everything, even failure; believe what's next will be better and we'll grow from what was, and that is a great way to live.

Faith is strengthened in several ways; you know what they are. Investing time and energy in these areas will reap dividends in the quest to fulfill our vision and maximize life. But the bigger game is that your examples and expressions of faith become so apparent they begin to grow the faith of those around you. *Something in your life requires you take a step in faith; take that step with complete confidence today.*

The Question: If I conducted a detailed account status of my faith in the various areas of my life, what would I find, and what would I do to increase it?

62. Loving Universally

We often choose to love *only* certain kinds of people to satisfy an addiction to relational convenience.

If you love those who love you, what credit is that to you? Even sinners love those who love them.

Luke 6:32

Throughout the difficulties and distractions of life, it's easy to forget the strategic nature of our Lord. From the universe, to the life he created, to the beauty of love and sex, down to the words he brought into existence for our language, there is brilliance in everything if you slow down enough to consider it.

Take the word *neighbor*, for example. Typically when we think of our neighbor, a few addresses on either side of our home come to mind, and perhaps the conviction that may come with how little we've invested into those relationships. *It does for me.* Regardless, our mindset about the term can be pretty limiting, especially if the nearest neighbor is five miles away. The New Testament Greek word translated as *neighbor* means "a friend," "any other person," and more that implies the same.[1] Seems to me that would make *everyone you are in the presence of.*

True theological revelation will always be
discovered by loving one another.

As it relates to love, God has closed all the loopholes, creating clear accountability and a directive to love everyone near us, despite whether it's convenient or comfortable. What's more brilliant is the diversity of people we are exposed to in a given day. You know, the ones we ignore simply because they look different, act different, or have personalities that rub us the wrong way.

We live in an ethnically, racially, socially diverse world and have a great opportunity to learn to love in a Christlike manner by getting rid of a popular practice called *selective love.* At times we may think that odd or irritating people who come into our sphere are there so we can practice our avoidance skills. *They're not.* We encounter all kinds of people as part of God's plan to help us embrace and thrive in diversity, which are ultimately necessary for our growth. We will also encounter a mixed grill of personalities in our life every day, each one God's perfect provision to practice love in a new and extraordinary way. It will cause us to reach deeply into the spirit of selflessness and will necessitate conversations with the Holy Spirit on how to attend to these relationships—relationships, by the way, that often become more meaningful and rewarding when we initiate effort toward them. *Invest a little more into your neighbors today.*

The Question: Who in my life do I tend to avoid that I could practice love on?

---

1. The NAS New Testament Greek Lexicon, s.v. "plesion," https://www.bible studytools.com/lexicons/greek/nas/plesion.html.

63. Presence That Ministers

> We all carry a presence that
> others experience.

Then Jesus again spoke to them, saying, "I am the Light of the world; he who follows Me will not walk in the darkness, but will have the Light of life."

John 8:12 NASB

Picture for a moment a recent event you attended. Pause and envision the event. Recount the way you walked into the room, and the mindset and heartset you brought with you. Was it optimistic, passionate, looking forward to the time? Or perhaps tentative, skeptical, fearful, or devoid of expectation, *nondescript*? Notice your contribution and your interaction during the event. Was it safe, slightly contrived, or did you participate with a sense of intentionality, clear about who you wanted to be and what you wanted to cause? Recall your focus. Was it on you and what you were doing or not doing right (*your image*) or was it on others and how you might serve the people and the event, if even with only your attitude? Overall, was it more *survive* or *thrive*, more taking or giving, more limitation or possibility? Most critically, was any thought or preparedness of heart exercised in advance of the event?

> If you want to join a great cause, be resolute, prepared, and intentional about what you are committed to cause, at all times. *That's a great cause.*

It is helpful to accept that attending any event without acknowledging the presence of God within us will likely result in our insecurities, entitlements, or awkwardness subtly or noticeably manifesting in the room. In contrast, what may be possible in a gathering will always improve by spending a short time becoming more aware of whose presence we carry, getting grounded in the geographic location of God. At times, God may seem distant simply because we've lost touch that he is not far away at all—even better, he is within us.

All gatherings, casual to critical in nature, will be well served if we maintain a sensitivity to God's presence in us and around us before and during the time, while remaining aware of how God might use us to impact the circumstances. It's that, or we end up focusing on all the issues of self that sabotage the beauty of what God desires for us to have in every experience. The simple connectedness to God's indwelling has an amazing ability to usher peace, joy, and opportunity into a gathering instead of bringing our own presence riddled with past baggage or the current load of life.

Now picture a room with people who have ALL chosen to be in full acknowledgment of the presence of God in them, around them, and in others. A room of people devoid of satisfying their own needs but instead practicing selflessness, caring for each other, and free from the social pressure common in gatherings. Now we're getting closer to heaven. *Walk, talk, and exude the presence that is already within you. Don't get in the way of it today.*

The Question: Do I spend time getting grounded before going into the presence of others so I can be confident and clear about God's presence in me?

64. God's Word versus Our Rhetoric

> It's always safer to connect people to God's truth instead of connecting them to our opinions.

All Scripture is God-breathed and is useful for teaching, rebuking, correcting and training in righteousness.

2 Timothy 3:16

If we were to count the times the words we shared with others came back void, it would be vast. In community settings, no matter how brilliant we are with our words, there's always some level of uncertainty when making a strong point to impact a conversation or agenda. We will always have a choice to share from a place of our own experiences, opinions, and knowledge base or share straight from God's Word with discernment and a caring heart. Both are opportunities, but one is God's Word and the other is a form of gambling—and we generally know it.

For instance, there have been occasions in group settings where I've shared a bit of my philosophy and snazzy wordplay on the evening's topic only to reap a room full of blank stares. Then my wife chimes in to save the day by gracefully and sensitively sharing a single relevant Scripture or story in the Bible on the same topic that ties to the conversation, makes the point clear, and is backed by God himself. The blank stares in the room turn to realizations and gratitude, and the conversation picks up momentum and moves to a meaningful place with context and an anchor. This is not a universal reality in all situations, but it's often a missed opportunity, because we are missing the biblical knowledge to contribute that way.

> To NOT be well versed in verses puts you in a
> position of weakness versus one of strength.

I think deep down we all desire to make a difference with others and all have ways of going about it. Sometimes we're on point, sometimes . . . *blank stares*. Other times we risk offending or shutting down conversation because our desire to appear knowledgeable and look good supersedes wise restraint. Regardless, there is a consistent, humble, and effective way to impact people's lives, and that is to know God's Word well enough to share it with others in conversations and times of need. Not as a Bible thumper but in offering considerations of what the Bible has to say about certain things and sharing with others the brilliance it contains. You don't have to be a wordsmith, great speaker, or slick communicator; just connect them to God's truth about what's what—gently and lovingly.

Using on- or off-line tools and apps, relevant chapters and verses on topics are a quick search away, and the Word of God is comprehensive. It covers every area of life in some form or another and can never be labeled as anything less than wisdom. There is a caveat to sharing God's Word, though. If you want someone to experience a full connection to God's truth, they should experience the love of Christ in your careful delivery, in the form of a loving heart that cares. Having Scriptures and biblical references in the memory queue not only gives us resolve when discussing life's challenging topics; committing to Scripture also gives us a diversity of tools to serve in any situation we are in. Even memorizing one verse a week adds up to fifty-two this year and more than five hundred in ten years. *Develop a Scripture memory plan today and be more effective in communication tomorrow.*

The Question: In times of teaching/exploring, do I get tempted to make it the "*me* show," or is there a simpler, less stressful way to just connect people to God's truth about the subject?

65. The Right Mix of Spiritual Disciplines

> Inconsistency in your spiritual disciplines will cause consistency in your stress level.

Not that I have already obtained all this, or have already arrived at my goal, but I press on to take hold of that for which Christ Jesus took hold of me. Brothers and sisters, I do not consider myself yet to have taken hold of it. But one thing I do: Forgetting what is behind and straining toward what is ahead, I press on toward the goal to win the prize for which God has called me heavenward in Christ Jesus.

Philippians 3:12–14

Our emotional strength and life effectiveness directly correlate with our spiritual disciplines of staying engaged with God. We stick gas in our car . . . *it goes,* food in our body . . . *it goes.* Yet sometimes we believe we can live a high-performance lifestyle with a casual diet of prayer, occasional visits into the Word, and worship when it's convenient. The result? We're forced to operate in our own strength, not the spirit of God, and we wind up suffering from our own lack of discipline. But it goes beyond that.

Curious about the spiritual disciplines of others, I set out on a journey to ask those I respect about their spiritual routine. I heard every kind of answer including a mix of Word, worship, and prayer for two hours to start every day, to no set pattern except a constant tapping into the things of God throughout the day, and everything in between. I've also seen people who share they have high degrees of commitment in their spiritual disciplines, but their lives and relationships are a mess. Then there are others who have no real "program" and yet they are thriving, joyful, and growing. That got me thinking that for each of us, there is a right mix of disciplines during certain seasons of life, and the inventory of available disciplines may need to expand outside the traditional Word, worship, and prayer into other areas that may not seem like spiritual disciplines simply because we haven't considered them that way.

> Discipline is when you turn down something you
> want to do for something you ought to do.

Some of the unconventional or uncategorized areas of spiritual discipline are these:

1. A constant dialogue with the Holy Spirit about all things in our life in the spare minutes and seconds of our day.
2. Gathering with other Christians to discuss God's words and what he may be doing in our lives and theirs.
3. Giving thanks to the Lord for what we've been given all throughout the day and perhaps having the insight and maturity to even thank him for the challenges in our life.

4. Opening ourselves up to the counsel of others so we can receive feedback in key areas of our life where we are locked up, lacking, or in a state of breakdown.

5. Being in a still, quiet place so we can experience moments of peace without an agenda, leaving room for God to place things on our heart and mind that need to be there.

6. Meditating on how God will use us as a tool of his grace, love, and impact.

These are just a few, but consider that blending them into the basics can breathe new life not only into the disciplines themselves but into every area of our lives. It would serve us well to have a conversation with God about integrating new areas of discipline to keep the old areas from feeling recycled or like an obligation or task.

The Question: Could my current spiritual disciplines use an effectiveness check, and is there room to integrate them into new areas during this season of my life?

66. Going Beyond Expectations

> Delivering what is expected is nothing special. Delivering beyond expectations should be the way of the believer.

If someone slaps you on one cheek, turn to them the other also. If someone takes your coat, do not withhold your shirt from them. Give to everyone who asks you, and if anyone takes what belongs to you, do not demand it back. Do to others as you would have them do to you.

If you love those who love you, what credit is that to you? Even sinners love those who love them. And if you do good to those who are good to you, what credit is that to you? Even sinners do that.

Luke 6:29–33

I'm certain you'll agree, *these days*, that it's a pleasant surprise when people actually fulfill their commitments to the level they say they will. I'm also sure you'll agree that it's even rarer when people deliver on their commitment and go beyond it to do something a little extra. Although it's the rare thing to do, God tells us to do just that. How amazing our relationships would be if we got creative with our commitments and integrated those little extras that surprise people and bring them smiles, gratefulness, and inspiration.

Relationships are kept together by **GLUE**:
Giving **L**ove **U**nceasingly & **E**xtravagantly.

In a world where average seems to be the norm, there is ample opportunity to stand out from the crowd. In Romans 12:1–2, God calls us not to be conformed to the world, and the word *conformed* here means "blend in." In other words, don't be dull in a world in need of vibrancy—God's vibrancy. Exemplary commitments, outstanding behaviors, extraordinary love, and a job beyond well done are part of that color and standing out. When you think of the brilliance behind God's call here, it all begins to make sense. To stand out and be noticed by others provides the opportunity to share where that commitment comes from, and perhaps what makes us different. It provides fertile evangelistic ground because the other has experienced a godly commitment through you, so the words you share will resonate and have the credibility to be heard with optimism, not skepticism.

The key is to realize that "beyond what is expected" doesn't mean do twice the work. As crazy as it seems, an extra 1 to 10 percent will generally capture the hearts of others; that creates the space for the relationship to move to a new place of trust, enjoyment, and durability. A little time spent with the Holy Spirit goes a long way here. A bit of collaboration on the creativity of "extra" will always bring something to our hearts that we can deliver. *Look around; everything and everyone in your sphere could use your little extra today.*

The Question: With those in my life, what would going beyond normal look like? Will I be a "go beyond" person or a "just enough to get by" person?

67. Theology Comes to Life

> Why is it you seek more meat, if you can't even deliver on the milk?

Brothers and sisters, I could not address you as people who live by the Spirit but as people who are still worldly—mere infants in Christ. I gave you milk, not solid food, for you were not yet ready for it. Indeed, you are still not ready.

1 Corinthians 3:1–2

Knowing that the human mind will never comprehend the full depths and mysteries of God gives us pause to reflect on the quest and purpose for amassing more biblical knowledge. Although what I just said may sound idiotic, even heretical, consider for a moment that the pinnacle of theological brilliance will never be found in an ability to debate and supposedly win a theological argument as much as to love God and others at a serious depth and win souls for Christ. That's the simplicity of complexity sifted down, where the purpose of theological knowledge shifts from what we get from it (that "knowledge puffs up" thing) to how we give and love abundantly through it.

Over the years I've heard many flippant comments from Christians about how seeker-sensitive churches are providing nothing but milk and there is nothing to be learned there except for the basics. Some of these self-purported Bible scholars regarded the church as doomed because it hadn't (in their eyes) reached their perceived level of theological acumen. And yet God uses scholars and intellectuals in mighty ways like he does all of us by working in and through our brokenness.

> The hunger for knowledge is a good thing until it begins
> to take precedence over our commitment to love.

Whenever the basics of loving God and loving others take a backseat to seeking more meat in a message, we run the risk of feeling superior to others. This tainted quest for knowledge (1 Cor. 13:1–3) can and generally does instill an ugly self-righteousness that will separate us from others and limit our capacity to be heard. It also runs the risk of being an escape from the two main mandates of our Christian walk. FACT: Loving God and loving others does not take great depths of knowledge, nor must we be theologians to engage with God and show love with extravagance. There are some, however, who feel that knowledge is a driver of intimacy. It certainly can be, and we should be in the Word daily, but it is not the only way to increase our capacity to show Christ's love to others. Frankly, to study is easy, and it can be a trap to be a recluse and avoid the primary, more selfless but more difficult commandments—many of which may be in dire need of our attention.

To love God and love others with sacrifice, excellence, and consistency is a high bar that accelerates our spiritual growth in ways that are almost unfathomable in comparison to head knowledge. It is also miraculous the way the Holy Spirit instills theological wisdom and understanding within us when we engage in acts of love toward God and others. It is this kind of wisdom that surpasses understanding, and it's the kind that people are drawn to instead of run from. *Show theological brilliance in how you love today.*

The Question: Is there a healthy balance of knowledge and love in your walk, and is love the foundation, or even the purpose, for seeking more biblical knowledge?

68. Removing Certain Sins from Our Lives

> Quitting something is usually *futile* until you have something to replace it with.

How can a young person stay on the path of purity?
By living according to your Word.

Psalm 119:9

Ultimately it is God who perfects and heals us. However, he gave us an asset called *free will* so we could participate in our walk with him at any level we choose. We can take a casual stance, letting our Christianity grow by osmosis, or we can maximize our time here on earth by integrating new disciplines and practices into our lives while removing obstacles that hinder our growth and effectiveness.

I'll take a risk here and assume most of us have an ongoing sin or two we need to stop, things that keep us from intimacy with God and others or that have us feeling subtle to serious shame or tension in our persona. Could be circumstantial sin, could be habitual, even addictive, but we know in our hearts we'd live better and be more effective Christians if these sins were a thing of the past instead of a liability in the present and a barrier to our future potential. We can become quite skilled at justifying our sins and disguising them so they seem less apparent to others, and even to ourselves. And yet the ramifications will remain substantial both internally and externally if we choose to live in ongoing sin. There's no getting away from that.

> Ongoing sin is a universal derailment device from all
> that we can be and everything that is meaningful while
> quietly distancing ourselves from God and others.

I've always believed it is near impossible to break any addiction, stronghold, or habit of sin unless we have something to replace it with that's of equal or greater value than what we derive from the sin itself. The idea of stopping any behavior without a new vision or value to focus on will drive the never-ending mental conversation of *I need to quit this.* Quit what? *This!* What? *This, you know—THIS!* Unfortunately, the quit-this-without-another-option strategy acts as a perpetual reminder to focus on the sin . . . rather than the new vision. In order to proactively assault whatever *this* is, we need to move from *this* to *that*: a new vision worth having. Proclaim (aloud) "I'm moving toward *THAT*."

This could be the commitment to move away from pornography to having a great sex life with your spouse, or moving away from gluttony to getting in the best shape of your life, or quitting drugs or alcohol to have a clear mind to achieve future goals. Having a vision that is greater than any sin in our lives is a great tool God can use to pull us away from the sin we're in and draw us into a new place of hope. In other words, the more effort you put into the new thing, the more you'll detach from the old. It's not a guarantee, of course, but consider the upside: even if you hold on to the old thing for God to deal with when he chooses, you still get the value that comes from integrating the new thing of value into your life. *Consider some replacement parts for habits, strongholds, or addictions today.*

The Question: What vision can replace the sin I have in my life and draw me away from it?

69. How Our Eyes Minister

> How do you look at people? It's worth taking a look at what they may see.

Your eye is the lamp of your body. When your eyes are healthy, your whole body also is full of light. But when they are unhealthy, your body also is full of darkness.

Luke 11:34

For some reason I've been paying attention to the facial expressions and eye contact of other believers lately. I've been considering my own as well. This choice was based on a comment that a friend of mine made to me, driving me to look closer at people as I interacted with them and to observe the way they engaged with others. What I saw was pretty interesting. Given there was enough break from whatever smartphone or screen some were glued to, I was able to see that there was a tension in people's looks. I noticed a disinterested "I need to get on with the next thing, let me get back to my technology, there's no opportunity here" look that was almost expressionless, robotic, abstract, and blasé with no real connection behind some of the expressions. It was almost as if, especially in customer service experiences, I was an inconvenience or obstacle to get past, not a life to minister to. I couldn't find much enthusiasm or real interest except on rare occasions when the person's attention and eye contact were focused, present, and inspiring.

Eye contact = I contact.

Have you ever considered how people experience you when you engage with them? How do they receive the authentic disposition of your true expressions? Do others see skepticism, disinterest, distraction, resignation, stress, and tension, or do they see acceptance, love, discernment, wisdom, hope, and peace? Although we may not give it much thought, our eyes are a big part of the process in building trust and rapport. They are always drawing people in or tuning them out. Our eyes are also one of the many reveals for where we are in our relationship with the Lord, and others can see that more clearly than we think. Proverbs 30:17 implies the eyes are the window to the soul, and in subtle yet powerful ways, the eyes reveal how vivid our sight on the Lord really is. Our eyes are affected by where we focus our hearts and minds—either on the Lord and all his blessings or ourselves and what may be missing.

Do our eyes say, "I am grateful to be eternally saved, living in the joy of the Lord and all his blessings," or do they say, "I'm marginally in touch with his blessings, too caught up in the natural realm to have eyes that shine with hope, joy, and God's presence"? In a very real way our eyes show either abundance or scarcity. A friend of mine once told me, "Dean, you can minister to someone with your eyes. You can connect them to God's love with a simple glance." I never forgot that. *Let your eyes indicate a state of true gratefulness today so that others can see the Lord in you.*

The Question: Will I take a few moments today to consider how my eyes are ministering to others?

70. Appreciating What's *Not* There

> Contentment in life often rests more
> on the absence of things.

And now these things remain, faith, hope and love, but the
greatest of these is love.

1 Corinthians 13:13

It was 4:00 a.m. when I heard a small cry come from the kitchen.
Faintly I heard my name: *"Dean."* I turned on the light, walked
into the kitchen, and found my wife, disoriented, slipping in a
large pool of blood and fighting to regain consciousness from an
internal hemorrhage that bled out. I ran to grab her, held her cold
body in my arms, and lowered her to the ground. As I was telling
her it would be okay, her eyes glazed over and I thought for a moment I'd lost her. After I uttered the words "No Lord, no, please
Lord" for about ten seconds, suddenly she regained consciousness.
It was the longest ten seconds of my life. I called 911, and shortly
a team of medics arrived and took us to the hospital.

After the nurses assured me she was in good hands and stable,
I went into an outdoor area where I could get a signal to call my

family and let them know what had happened. I couldn't reach anyone. Standing there thinking, staring off in the distance, I realized three things in that moment. One was the intense love I had for my wife. Second was the most profound state of gratefulness to God I'd ever experienced. Third was that nothing else in the world mattered in that moment other than love and gratefulness. All the things I held as vital in the busyness of my life had vaporized into nothingness. Although I'd just gone through the most traumatic event of my life, I said to myself with a greater sense of clarity than I'd ever had, "Ahhhhh, so this is what heaven is like." This was the peace that surpasses all understanding that I'd heard about so often. And yet the only thing that occurred other than a traumatic life event was that my focus on love and gratefulness created the diminution of everything else in my life, except what was in the moment. Love and gratefulness—I could not see past that—and it was heavenly.

A few seconds of semi-focused thought on an issue
are generally useless. Real revelations come in about
a minute of focused, uninterrupted contemplation.

Since that time, I have paid closer attention to what happens emotionally and spiritually when I focus in real time on the things of the Lord. Although not as intense as that moment at the hospital, there is a direct correlation to the absence of stress, anger, frustration, tension, uncertainty, and fear when my focus is the spiritual, not the natural. It's as if every potential negative "anything" gets minimized or eliminated with every spiritual recognition; the closer God's principles are in my mind, the further into the distance those undesirable things travel. And when I invest enough meditative thought, negative things become more distant from my presence . . . until, of course, I let my mind relax into a state of laziness, lighting up a vacancy sign for Satan to check in and bring grief into the rooms of my mind.

It's wise to take a day or two and write down our thought inventory to see where our focus is. Is it more on the spiritual or the natural? If stress, pressure, tension, and fear are present, you can be almost certain the focus is more on the natural. *Take a moment to reconnect to some spiritual principles today.*

The Question: How in tune with blessings am I in the various areas of my life? Is there more room to focus on those so the stress and tension become blurred?

71. The Value of Planning

Plan to hang out with God.
Hang out with God to *plan.*

In their hearts humans plan their course,
but the LORD establishes their steps.

Proverbs 16:9

It's funny (but then again, not) that we will ask God's input in basic situations but don't include God or spend time in serious contemplation, prayer, and meditation when planning some of the biggest initiatives, seasons, and dreams of our lives. Then a week, a month, a year later when one of our plans crumbles, we reach out to God to discuss the details, cry out, or worse—position ourselves as a victim of the collapse.

Developing a plan without collaborating with God will
often have you accelerating straight backward.

One of the promises we tend to forget is that God's consulting arm is always within reach, and the all-knowing, all-comforting, all-directing nature of the Holy Spirit is available to help set a solid foundation and a clear path for anything on our hearts. He is also there to guide us to seek out others, so we can capitalize on that "wisdom in a multitude of counselors" principle to help us plan for the highest and best use of our time, resources, and energy. It's really a stewardship issue over matters that affect us and often have a high impact on those in our care . . . *more than we may think.*

Just a guess, but it might help determine whether our plans are something we *should do* (along with the how, when, and with whom) if we align with the One who created the blueprint for our lives *before* the beginning of time. Too often we get so wrapped up in the perceived brilliance of our own plans and ideas that the voices of others (who God speaks through as well) are minimized or ignored because *we* know best: and in some cases . . . *we might.* But to have confirmation from God and from others—as well as guidance and an open channel of communication—is the way of a true steward, in contrast to a blind optimist who stumbles from plan to plan with little fruit to show for it.

I've seen and personally experienced plans built on the foundation of self-drive, and they are visions destined to rarely be fulfilled. They are generally a grease-on-a-glass-floor experience offering little or no traction and plenty of discomfort along the way. Not that the experience won't create value through learning (God will use it) but in most cases these solo launches of lunacy are time-consuming, expensive lessons that could have been avoided by taking the time to access the Holy Spirit and the counsel of others. God desires that we govern wisely over our visions, passions, goals, and time. *Make him part of your plans today. He made you part of his.*

The Question: At what level am I currently inviting God and others into my dreams and visions? Is there opportunity to access more wisdom and guidance on the things I do?

72. Receiving More from Church

> Will it be of more value to look at the church as a provision for you or to see yourself as a provision for the church?

For we are God's handiwork, created in Christ Jesus to do good works, which God prepared in advance for us to do.

Ephesians 2:10

Ask most people to get brutally honest about their church experience and you'll discover a range of subtle discontentment to all-consuming frustration: *The worship's too short (or too long). The music's too loud. The message was too soft (or too condemning, or too long). They didn't make me feel welcome. There's no place for me to be involved.* On and on it goes.

The church is not supposed to be a one-way delivery system for our happiness or our fulfillment; life in the church was not designed this way. But for some reason this is the expectation many have settled on—and if they can't have the church of their dreams, the nightmare begins. It becomes a negative experience that will have churchgoers church-hopping, church-bashing, or church-quitting, never discovering the perfect place. But that's usually because these kinds of churchgoers haven't ever discovered their true place in the church.

Churches are comprised of people,
and people are fallible. Do the math.

Like most organizational experiences, your church experience is broken up into parts that make up a whole. No single part will provide enough value to give you complete contentment in the long haul. For example, on a good day the pastor will deliver about 20 percent value in your experience, the worship perhaps another 15 to 25 percent. The hallway flyby fellowship adds maybe another 10 percent, leaving some percentage for miscellaneous things. These percentages fluctuate to extreme levels, as humans are involved throughout the experience. But either way it leaves a pretty big percentage gap, and the gap will always be filled by whether or not we are using our inherent gifts and abilities to serve the church body. If there were any one attribute that could be the great equalizer and fulfiller of the church experience, *serving* would be it.

If at any point you are not adding value to your church via the gifts you possess, you are missing out on a key experience that church was meant to provide. Pastors change, worship morphs over time, and people come and go, but the one sustainable area of value in the church that can be relied on will always be found in our gifts being put to use. It brings a balance to the church experience that lasts. In fact, I've never seen anyone actively experiencing the fruits of their calling in a church body have the time, energy, focus, or desire to complain about the things that may be missing or what they see as wrong. Fulfillment is found in a *fully integrated experience*, not in isolated categories so easily judged because we think the church is not giving us what we need, or because others have an off day and fail to deliver to our standard. In a word, the church will give us what we need as we pour more into the church. It's the difference between being a churchgoer and a church-grower. *Look at the percentages of value you are getting from church, and see how you can add to fill the gap.*

The Question: Do I have a healthy receive/give balance in my church life that adds up to an experience I'd never get tired of?

PS: If the church you're going to is unwilling to create space for you to use your gifts, maybe it's time to seek out a place where you can be used.

73. Freedom from Idols

> Do I spend more time meditating
> on the things of God or more time
> medicating myself with idols?

You shall not make for yourself an image in the form
of anything in heaven above or on the earth beneath
or in the waters below.

Deuteronomy 5:8

Imagine a life free from idols or attachments, living in a way in which no person or thing on earth can influence the flow of what God is doing spiritually in our life. Feel its freedom, the lightness of thought, the richness of heart, and a pure joy that is hindered by nothing. Now consider your current life. Perhaps it's filled with conditions to complete freedom that only idols can solve. Feel the dependency and the effort it takes to package the idols so they seem less obvious and almost innocent, when in fact if we are honest with ourselves, they comprise much of what we disguise as fulfillment. I know, as this is the one area I have struggled with, shared with others openly about, and received confirmation that this issue is widespread today. It takes only about five minutes of thought to see the gravity of discontentment we would experience if certain things were ripped immediately from our lives. There are many and they are unique to each of us.

> As for those who say they don't have an issue with idolatry, the need to be perfect is one idol that comes to mind.

It's no revelation that as believers we walk through life longing to minimize our dependency on money, pride, possessions, power, and others' approval. But upon close inspection, we may find much of our energy is spent keeping idols on some form of life support to satisfy self and distract from the pain that manifests when our identity is found more in idols than in Christ. Weary and tired, the day done, we sleep intermittently as we try to get rest, but are agitated by the prodding presence of idols of all shapes and sizes. Morning comes and before we can clear our minds to see God and the value in that intimacy, the allure of current or new idols captures our thoughts and the cycle continues—until, of course, we change our focus from what is temporal . . . *to what is eternal*. Although there are a number of ways to overcome various strongholds in our Christian walk, idolatry is one area where there is only one answer: finding our core fulfillment with God alone.

The beginning *of the end* of idolatry will always be found in moving to a deeper relationship with God and uncovering the richness so that we never feel we are dependent on idols as a means for our fulfillment. Candidly, there is no other way to find lasting contentment in our life, for he is eternal while everything else is not. And as we further embrace the innate beauty found in our identity in Christ, the outcome of that awareness weakens the stronghold of idols. In comparison to the blessings we discover in him, idols will no longer compare. As we grow closer to God, the attachments will distance themselves, the juggling of idols will stop, and we will be freer to move through life without the weight and pressure idolatry brings. *Take an idol inventory today and see what reveals itself.*

The Question: Is there enough of the fruit of the Spirit in your relationship with God to make idols seem less attractive and in proper perspective?

74. Seeing Problems as Opportunities

Don't let your test *not* turn into a testimony.

He replied, "Whether he is a sinner or not, I don't know. One thing I do know. I was blind but now I see!"

John 9:25

When I see someone (including myself) get emotionally overtaken by a problem in life, I'm inclined to ask a simple question: Whose doctrine are you working from as the basis in dealing with the problem: God's or your own? The distinction is vital; if the habit is to default away from any of God's perspective of dealing with a trial, we lose our anchor. The waves of emotion drown out God's voice and what he has to say throughout the challenge. It's the difference between being locked into the symptoms of the trial, which stops insight and possibility, and freely seeing *through* the trial to the blessings that will be derived from it and what it could mean to our growth as believers.

Either you own and control problems or
problems own and control you.

Whenever we leverage a trial in a godly manner, there will always be a story worth sharing—one that will make a difference with others due to our governing through the trial with Christ-like mind and heart. Some of the most authentic, impactful, and transformational words that can come from a Christian's mouth are their testimony of how God worked in a difficult circumstance or test. It starts by understanding that the test you're in is *nothing more than a testimony that hasn't played out yet*. It's a stand of faith to believe that God has complete control of the reins and will work ALL things for the good of those who seek him and are called according to his purpose. Next is to be in a healthy state of contemplation of what God wants to accomplish during the test: the lives he wants to touch, the initiatives he wants to forward, and how he wants you to grow through the trial. A test can be held as a testimony from the second it rears its difficult yet wonderful head. We just need to combat our own thoughts and dwell on God's promise that a trial is ultimately an asset; no matter how bad the circumstances, you will have a platform to share how God worked at the end of it.

Trials pass, they always do, so as shared earlier the real victory can never be defined by whether we get through the trial or not, but HOW we get through it. *That is the victory.* As Christians who desire to mature consistently, we should never waste a trial, as they are a precious resource for the believer to move to new levels of faith and confidence in life. Yet the value can be lost if they are not seen in their true light from the onset. *Envision what the testimony will look like from a trial you are in and participate to that end today.*

The Question: What is my default when trials hit—to embrace them and be an instrument of God, or to be a victim of the trial?

75. The Power of Our Voice

> Give voice to the things of your heart: an audible, intentional, and yes, even LOUD voice!!!

When the trumpets sounded, the army shouted, and at the sound of the trumpet, when the men gave a loud shout, the wall collapsed; so everyone charged straight in, and they took the city.

Joshua 6:20

The conversations we have with ourselves take place in our mind hundreds of times daily. Some of those contain healthy, uplifting dialogue, and some thoughts subvert and discourage us. Because they are only internal conversations, we minimize their impact— we label them as mere thoughts. But the recurrence of repetitive negative thinking demands a closer look and an active stance, as it can remove the joy from our lives quicker than we may think.

This leads us to a rarely discussed life-changing activity called a *verbal proclamation*. Most proclamations we make about the desires of our heart, position in the world, and the nature of our identity in Christ are kept quietly within our mind and held timidly because we're not comfortable going beyond that. In other words, when we think a negative thought, we generally think it's adequate to combat it with a positive thought. That's a good start, but it's a fairly passive approach limited in its power and authority, and the thoughts are processed in the swirling confetti of our minds. It's a pretty crazy place in our minds, as you know.

> When you think something, only your mind hears it. When you give voice to something, your mouth says it, your mind acknowledges it, and your ears listen to it. That's two-thirds more power.

Whether we're taking new ground in life, combating old thinking, or just desiring to get realigned or connected to our potential in Christ, we will benefit by going beyond rearranging old thoughts to giving a new, clear, *audible voice* to the things we desire to become real; scream them at the top of your lungs if you must. Seems silly until you practice it and discover that words spoken out loud have many times more impact than words thought in the mind, and they act as accelerants to progress and growth. The act of voicing our words aloud into the physical universe and unto God gives proclamation a different physiological and spiritual dynamic. We speak it, then hear it with our ears, then feel it in our mind and spirit in ways that could never be experienced solely by pondering it. The benefit is immediate, which makes a test run worthwhile.

Proclamation is a declaration that will drive notable endurance into our lives, taking our faith in what we're proclaiming to a new place. And if you want to add a higher degree of effectiveness in this area, proclaim things out loud and provide specific details about your proclamation in front of a group of close friends, acquaintances, and associates to cast more light and bring more accountability to what you share. *Consider the value of proclamations today, public or private.*

The Question: Will I take a moment and proclaim several aspects of who I am in Christ and/or things I will accomplish in him, or will I remain silent and just ponder?

76. Removing Pressure from Life

Simplify life with an audience of one.

Now fear the LORD and serve him with all faithfulness. Throw away the gods your ancestors worshiped beyond the Euphrates River and in Egypt, and serve the LORD.

Joshua 24:14

Have you ever stopped to take notice of how people affect you with their approval or disapproval? Your peace, joy, and happiness hang in the balance of whether you act right, dress right, say it right, do it right, and get it right . . . *or not*. Metaphorically, it's like juggling cannonballs to keep in the constant favor of those around you, and it's a clear victory of the enemy when your worth rests on whether you're pleasing or not pleasing people—living *or dead*. I operated in this bondage most of my life, but I now know it's a "fool-time" job with no real value other than temporary bits of self-worth that don't last very long.

When we choose to love others rather than try to impress them, that in itself will leave the best impression.

It's worth an occasional look at the actual payoff we receive in striving to please others, and also to check the motives of our heart while doing so. Motives bounce back and forth between looking good, feeling self-worth and acceptance, and occasionally other, godlier motives that are driven by a servant's heart. Regardless, there will always be disappointment, because people are involved. We will be misinterpreted, misunderstood, undervalued, and judged for our actions whether done from a pure heart or not, so it makes the endeavor of pleasing man unsustainable in the long run.

There is another option, and that is to focus on serving God—an audience of one. Engaging with others based on God's instruction, wisdom, and prompting of the Holy Spirit makes a life more simplified and provides insight on how to most effectively serve those in our care. Following his lead and saying to ourselves, "What would serve God in this circumstance?" takes away much of the guesswork of how others may respond and makes being with others a pleasure rather than a performance. It's a call to a higher degree of intimacy and sensitivity, so your acts of service stay relevant and consistent, and you'll improve your spiritual and relational awareness in the process.

But there is a caveat here. When God says people will know us by our love for one another, he's indicating that evaluating how we are loving others is a wise practice so we can refine our sensitivity to God's leading and the relevance in how we serve. He wants us to pay close attention to our fruit and take measure; if outcomes are bad, he desires that we examine why our attempts fell flat or had less-than-desirable results. In contrast, if things are showing up well, it acts as an encouragement to do more of what's working. *Place more consideration on what would serve God, and see what shows up in others today.*

The Question: Am I ready to give up the tireless job of pleasing others? Instead will I use God's Word as the foundation to please God, and in turn increase the opportunities to bring value to others?

77. Every Commitment Matters

> Many claim to have character when at best they have circumstantial integrity.

All you need to say is simply "Yes" or "No"; anything beyond this comes from the evil one.

Matthew 5:37

If there is a notable trait among Christians that turns nonbelievers off to the idea of Christianity, it's that some Christians don't practice what they preach, nor do they follow through on the commitments they make to others—they simply don't keep their word. Unfortunately, lack of integrity is an everyday problem in the church, and yet there seems to be little spoken about it. Perhaps that's because many who could speak on the subject have a life riddled with small or large broken commitments, and given their position, the hypocrisy and potential exposure would be too much.

Breakdown in integrity is more common than we think due to a twisted notion that "I don't always have to keep my word because I fall under God's grace," or some other out-of-context biblical rationalization where God, our position, or our status is used as a veil to cover our dysfunction. The world looking in on Christianity, however, doesn't have God's level of grace and doesn't care about our excuses. And if we are to be a good representation of Christianity, we should stop with the rationales or blame and deliver on what we say we will do every time, without fail. At the very least we should have the courtesy to renegotiate a potential broken commitment long before the deadline, instead of the norm of blowing it off.

> Integrity is NOT installed in our being when we become Christians; salvation is, but as for integrity, that's not a one-time installation but a never-ending activation.

The reality: most people you talk to will boldly proclaim they have integrity, and yet most people say there isn't enough of it. There's an obvious disconnect here, and it stems from the nature and true definition of integrity. *Integritas*, the Latin word for integrity, alludes to the totality of our belief system working together in all areas of life at all times. So to have integrity means that every area of our character in life is in alignment and is executed with consistency and predictability. In contrast, *circumstantial integrity* is keeping commitments in areas of your life where you gain advantage or it's convenient and generally doesn't require too much sacrifice. It is a form of feeling-based integrity that remains the common path for most, and it's clearly out of sync with a total integrated system of character as defined in the Bible.

Even though circumstantial integrity may seem to give us more comfort and convenience, what it makes us is unreliable, unpredictable, and hypocritical in the eyes of others . . . *even ourselves* over time. The truth is, no one can say they own integrity—it's a practice and a process, not a possession. For those who want the solidity of spirit that goes with exercising integrity, they must give a full commitment that ignores feelings and moods and keep their commitments despite the circumstances. God keeps all his commitments. His Word is everything, as is ours. *Keep every commitment you make from here on out or simply stop making them.*

The Question: Do I keep every commitment I make, whether large or small, or do I rest on excuses as a means to escape my responsibility?

78. The Opportunity of the Seemingly Insignificant

> God isn't too busy for the small things, and the small things are bigger than we think.

Do not be anxious about anything, but in every situation, by prayer and petition, with thanksgiving, present your requests to God.

Philippians 4:6

When we think about our problems and what might require the support of others, we often minimize the smaller—or what we might label as unimportant—problems. So we rarely reach out to others with such trivial things. Certainly, others don't have time to contend with the abundance of small on-the-fly realities we deal with. True, for the most part they don't, and they may not take them too seriously after the first ten or so. But God does, and he is very serious about dealing with anything, of any size—especially if it keeps you from experiencing fulfillment in Christ.

What's encouraging here is that God's infinite bandwidth, comfort, wisdom, and problem-solving brilliance are available in the blink of a sigh or a cry. Aside from forming the universe, he made well over eight million living creatures in six days, including two highly deluxe versions named Adam and Eve, billions of stars and planets, and oh, I almost forgot gravity and *much more*. I'm pretty sure he's got the time and capacity to deal with anything you can throw his way—big or small.

It's a simple practice that will become a highly valuable habit when you invite God into an ongoing conversation on day-to-day stuff: the hard lunch with an old friend, the broken relationship, the business meeting, the unforgiveness in your heart, the conversation with your spouse, what to get for their birthday, the parent/teacher conference, etc. Typically, God's hotline is called and the Holy Spirit is summoned when disease gets diagnosed, the affair is exposed, the addiction is discovered, the accident happens, or death's door knocks. These seem to be the triggers that drive us to put 888-GOD-4HLP on speed dial and call with the utmost consistency. But it's not just the occasional big thing that God wants to use to bring us into communion with him; it's the ongoing "everything": *constant communion.*

Small things add up to big impact. Like little overindulgences add up to a massive heart attack.

FACT: life gets more unhealthy and unproductive when the ongoing day-to-day small things are not carried out with godly collaboration and wisdom. As I shared in an earlier point, when executed in our own strength, these small go-it-alone issues pile up and climb onto our attitude and emotions, and what were once seemingly meaningless things bond together to form an insurmountable burden. As a result, we wind up searching for a spiritual boost but rarely tap into God's strength to deal with these current issues, let alone the small and/or big things coming soon to a situation near us. Beyond the occasional catastrophe call, God desires continual dialogue and interaction with him in ALL things. He wants us to access his innovation, wisdom, comfort, and strength perpetually, not occasionally. He wants us in rhythm and step with his power at all times so no matter what comes our way, big or small, we will be in a predisposition of strength to steward over it with the utmost resolve and he will be glorified. *Experience the brilliance of having a quick chat on the small things today.*

The Question: Are you in the habit of dialoguing with God about all things or waiting for the unpredictable big thing that may or may not come?

79. Praying with Authenticity

It's a prayer . . . not a *performance.*

> And when you pray, do not be like the hypocrites, for they love to pray standing in the synagogues and on the street corners to be seen by others. Truly I tell you, they have received their reward in full.
>
> Matthew 6:5

Prayer is a personal thing more than a professional aptitude. In light of that, it should be more of an authentic expression or appeal from our heart than a spotlight to step into. Not to say that we are all actors. But it's worth a look at the various circumstances we operate in to see what levels of embellishment or accentuation we put into our prayer and measure whether it moves us closer to or further from authenticity. Candidly, less-authentic prayers that are more performance based or intended to impress or please others are worth putting into storage for the remainder of our life.

Confession time: I've prayed in a multitude of ways over the years. I've done what I call the Holy Roller Coaster Prayer, where my volume goes up and down and down and up from window-breaking decibels to near silent. On more occasions than I care to admit, I've facilitated the Counseling Prayer, where I'd break out tools and start wrenching in people's heads with assumptions, concepts, and teaching and disguise it as a prayer. Then there was the Dictionary Prayer, where I wouldn't stop until I'd used every word in the dictionary because I wanted to hear myself talk. Of course, there was the infamous Sermon Prayer, and on and on. I can only ask forgiveness from God and others for a subtle-to-serious need every now and then to find my worth in the performance of a prayer rather than just being real.

When praying in public or private,
pray at the pace of authenticity.

I cannot label these versions of prayers I've described as bad for others, as everyone is unique, but in full disclosure relating to my own absurdity at times, I rarely (if ever) performed one of these stylistic prayers alone in a room with God—*only in public.* Honestly, I can't even imagine how bizarre that would be to myself or anyone else who happened to be in earshot if I did.

The unfortunate part of any performance-oriented prayer designed to incite emotion or create hype is that it often distracts people and gets them too caught up in the show to be authentically aligned to the prayer itself. The calamity is that these prayers move at the rhythm of the performance and not at the pace and reverence of the Holy Spirit (or perhaps, sensitivity to others). It's quite rare when you hear someone give reference and consideration as they're praying, humbly paying close attention to God's leading in the process. These authentic, reverent prayers devoid of performance are refreshing and relatable for all. They keep the focus where it should be, on God and not the person praying. *Pray with reverence and authenticity today.*

The Question: Do you pray from a humble and contrite spirit with little or no focus on self, or do your prayers lean toward performance?

80. Making a Great Day

> What we bring into our day is a choice
> as much as what we leave out.

Be very careful, then, how you live—not as unwise but as
wise, making the most of every opportunity, because the
days are evil. Therefore do not be foolish, but understand
what the Lord's will is.

Ephesians 5:15–17

Imagine walking up to someone and asking how they are doing,
and they respond with, "Well, I'm trying to deal with all the things
going on in my life, in one day." Your first thought is that you've
never heard anyone say that out loud before. Your next thought is,
What a stressful/impossible way to live! But your most alarming
thought is, *I wonder if I do that?*

An honest look may reveal that our minds bring more into a
day than is necessary and more than we could ever contend with.
What energy, focus, and emotional strength might be depleted
from the resources we have when we try to conquer all of life with

a series of random, unintentional thought fragments that give us more stress than progress?

If you consider the empathic nature of God when he tells you that every day you live will contain some version and volume of trouble, it can help you appreciate the need to allocate your human resources wisely, surrender what you cannot control within a day, and let life unfold without trying to solve everything at once. This perspective brings a peace to be able to contend readily with what is before us rather than carrying the weight of an entire life into current situations and feeling half exhausted from the mental baggage we drag into them.

Trusting that God's perfect plan includes a pace, direction, and control of our overall life will free up mental, emotional, and spiritual capital. Then we can deal with anything that comes our way in a day and leave extra room to think peacefully and freely about the things of tomorrow, if we choose. The other pearl in this principle is that it provides the space for us to be fully present to others without being absorbed by the burdens and distractions that cause us to be detached while in their presence. You've been with people like this; they're partially in the conversation, intermittently listening, nodding in politeness, but not fully engaged or rewarding to be with.

> To worry about a problem not solved will
> not get that problem resolved.

Our mind is a powerful tool. We have the capacity to think ourselves directly out of the present moment, or we can stay engaged in the moments and seconds of the day with everything and everyone in focus except the troubles and challenges of our life. When we stay present within the day, many thoughts that derail our peace, joy, productivity, and relationships are removed, making way for freedom in thought that somehow seems to bring resolve and hope to all areas and times of life . . . broken or not. *Be completely present in today and see what baggage doesn't show up.*

The Question: Am I carrying the burden of too many things into the day that I'm in?

81. The Nature of Offenses

> As for the so-called personal attack, nothing is personal. *Nothing!!!*

Bear with each other and forgive one another if any of you has a grievance against someone. Forgive as the Lord forgave you.

Colossians 3:13

We've all been betrayed, attacked, and slandered. The world we live in is an offensive one, riddled with sin both inside the church and out. Offense is open for business 24/7, so escaping the current and future onslaught of attacks (whether brought on by our own behavior or not) is futile. Only these questions matter when offenses come: Who will I be? How will I handle it? What spiritual condition will I be in to thrive through the offense? Without a decision to be a victor over offenses, your emotions and attention will remain wrapped up in the epicenter of them. It's always better to be holding any offense with peace, resolve, and optimism.

> Offense has no aim, it just happens to land
> on whoever is in front of its despair.

Fortunately, there are spiritual perspectives we can hold that drive resistance to the spiritual warfare that accompanies offenses. One of those is a simple dismissal of the idea that personal attacks exist; *they don't*. Our capacity to withstand the onslaught of assaults in life will increase if we accept that it's impossible for something to be personal. Claiming an attack to be directed solely at us is an illusion and a subtle form of self-flattery that we're actually important enough for someone to set out to invest their hatred and undone stuff into *only us*. Nobody is that important, and personal attacks have little to do with us but everything to do with someone who is simply working out their dysfunctions; we just happen to be the ones in their presence at the time, so we choose to take it personally.

But we don't have to. Trust me, there are others who reap the whirlwind of their breakdowns, behaviors, and betrayal, making these things a completely impersonal and unpredictably dispersed by-product of a person's stronghold depending on their mood and circumstance. The peace that comes with acknowledging the impersonal nature of attacks (no matter how personal they may look) removes confusion, adds compassion toward others, and multiplies our strength to help them through their dysfunctions—while taking limited or no ownership of their brokenness and experiencing less impact from their behavior.

As believers, it is never others who manage the control panel of our mindset and emotions, but us and God. This is an important distinction, because it positions you to hold others as powerless in subverting any value from your life, regardless of their offense. God's Word is clear that in his refuge there is strength, and in the eye of any storm there is calm for those who choose to co-control the emotions of their life with God and not others. *Today, reframe any offenses as impartial and impersonal and move to make a difference rather than make others pay.*

The Question: Do I get so emotionally unstable when offended by someone that I end up being useless to serve them, or do I become a source of strength?

82. Speaking with Power and Authority

> Discovering new ways and words to improve communication is *intelligence*. To discover a new heart behind the words you use . . . is *wisdom*.

Create in me a pure heart, O God,
    and renew a steadfast spirit within me.

Psalm 51:10

Knowing that relationships are created, developed, and sustained based largely on communication should move us to consider the myth of "sticks and stones may break my bones, but words will never hurt me." I'd prefer to stick to a more true-to-life quote that perhaps you've heard, one that has proven true over the centuries: that the pen [a metaphor for words] is mightier than the sword. Words have the ability to start wars and stop them, abolish hatred and usher in love, facilitate healing, bring relationships together or push them apart, and of course, be used to share the Word of God to minister to others (or, if wrongly delivered, turn them into adversaries of Christianity).

Words matter, and for the Christian they are the foundation of our witness and the resonance of our hearts—which is why the heart, tone, and manner in which we deliver our words is so important.

Although delivery has importance, manufactured eloquence and practiced polish in verbal communication is dying a slow death in today's world, as is data regurgitation and slick delivery. People, especially the upcoming generations, aren't easily moved by what we say or how well we say it but by our conviction and our authenticity when we're sharing.

> When communicating, the right motive with the right heart drives the right words in the right order in the right tone at the right time.

The effective communicators and difference makers in the world are clear about what they desire to cause in the hearts and minds of those they are speaking with, *specifically*. They are cognizant not so much of what they are going to say but of who they will be while communicating. They position themselves as a vessel to be used, not a show to be performed. They believe with every ounce of faith they have that God will do a great work in every conversation regardless of how good they may sound or how well they said something, simply because they cared with the heart of Christ and they were authentic in their approach. They focus mostly on being conversationally relevant instead of on being conversationally competent and impressive. As a result, the words they say resonate, make a positive impression on the other, and are received with fewer barriers of guardedness, skepticism, or suspicion. *Consider the heart from which you speak today and watch what gets spoken.*

The Question: What would my communication to others look like if I put a godly heart behind everything I said? Wow!

83. Not Giving . . . Takes

> Those who don't tithe may rationalize
> that it is not slighting God, but
> it will slight opportunity.

"Bring the whole tithe into the storehouse, that there may be food in my house. Test me in this," says the LORD Almighty, "and see if I will not throw open the floodgates of heaven and pour out so much blessing that there will not be room enough to store it."

Malachi 3:10

Tithing is a sensitive topic. Perhaps because money is linked to our faith in what God will provide like no other thing. That is, of course, until we experience a health crisis where money plays second fiddle in the "whether God will provide" arena. Regardless, while our health is in order, money ranks among the most important resources to the *average* human. Good thing we are called to extraordinary—meaning *beyond the average human*—in every aspect of our life.

Tithing is not like gambling. It's a form of investing with the right motive: dividends are not speculative but cumulative.

If for whatever reason you are not giving 10 percent of your income to God, I have only three words for you: *consider starting somewhere*. If I can't convince you giving 10 percent creates blessing beyond belief, and you can't take the leap to trust God's "test me on tithing" promise, I can only ask that you start small, phase in consistent giving, consider scalability, and evaluate as you grow. I am certain you'll wish you'd started this practice when you opened that first lemonade stand or sold your first baseball card for a profit. *I wish I had*. Although there is the Old Testament/ New Testament controversy over whether believers should tithe, I'll go out on a limb here (not really) and say that God appreciates obedience to the call. Regardless of theology, God loves and honors giving of any size, as do the churches and ministries we support. In many ways, the ministries we sow into are in a rhythm of growth that requires a predictable cash flow to run the organization and plan for the future. We are the natural provision for that, and it's when *we get in that rhythm with them* that giving becomes both a habit and a blessing for all concerned.

Over the years, I've heard from pastors I know that about 5 to 10 percent of the church gives 10 percent consistently, and the rest give low amounts sporadically, which is unfortunate. I'm sure if the world were looking in on this low number, they'd view our conviction as faint and absent of commitment. It doesn't take a genius to see that if 100 percent of the church tithed 10 percent we could more effectively evangelize the planet, make a big dent in hunger and homelessness, and impact dozens of other world issues. But I also believe if we started small, we could make a substantial difference immediately. Don't despise a small beginning in giving; exercise it, realize it, and most critically, enjoy how God will honor your heart in the process. *Give from a place of new faith today.*

The Question: Have I fully tested the principal of God's blessing on the tithe, or will I go to my grave never quite knowing what may have come to life had I engaged in the practice?

84. Seeing Other Believers in Transformation

> That friend, colleague, partner, or relative we are judging is changing and growing, just like we are.

Do not judge, and you will not be judged. Do not condemn, and you will not be condemned. Forgive, and you will be forgiven.

Luke 6:37

You've probably noticed that you are a different person today than you were five years ago. In fact, if you look back long enough, you'll see the subtle and macro changes over time have added up to a person who has grown pretty far from who you used to be. Thank God and his faithfulness in drawing us closer to his likeness and further from our old selves. You'd think the awareness of our own transformation would have us filled with a never-ending supply of grace, empathy, and compassion toward others who are in the process of change, despite what they said or did. And yet, at times we look at other believers with such disdain, skepticism, and judgment that if our thoughts were spoken aloud they would do great harm—and yet, *they already are doing great harm*, perhaps more so, by being kept inside.

I feel an incredible sense of Christian adolescence when I look at fellow believers in their current state instead of considering who they are becoming in Christ. Caught up in judgment and self-righteousness, I separate myself from any real relationship with them and sabotage any potential work God can do through me—all because I'm too immature in the moment to appreciate where God has them on their walk, who they are becoming in Christ, and the real truth . . . that they are *already perfected in him.*

It's wise to remember that everyone exists
in a process of transformation.

The issue here is that in my ignorantly limited mindset, I am seeing them in the natural realm, not the eternal realm, and I conveniently keep forgetting that *I'm currently living in an eternal realm, where everything can be seen through a godly lens.* At times in my life I have been graced to be with people who believed in me, saw me in light of God's perfecting nature, and engaged with me as if I were complete, not broken. There was something special in these people that was undeniably different from almost every other person I'd met. Their presence brought with it peace, and there was an ease of being with them that created the space for great things to happen relationally, emotionally, and spiritually. I remember these rare people, some dead and some still living, with a fondness that is unmatched, recounting their way of being as truly Christlike—and from a maturity standpoint, way ahead of many others.

Contrary to a pessimistic worldview, there is a stress-free way to be with all fellow believers. To see past who they are, how they look, and the way they act, and to take a stand for who they are becoming in Christ, is to be in a place of tremendous influence and intimacy. It's a stand that allows us a never-ending stream of opportunities to use our God-given gifts and hold people in a light that represents their true changing nature. *See others in a place of hope and clarity, not hopelessness and disparity, today.*

The Question: Do I interact with people in light of how I see them in the natural realm or who they are becoming in Christ?

85. Serving to Experience God

> We all have a place where we
> experience God most.

My ears had heard of you,
but now my eyes have seen you.

Job 42:5

To understand that God is present in all things, circumstances, and conversations suggests that it is not God who needs to make himself more present to us but we who must position ourselves to expand our awareness of God. I've always been fascinated with how Christians derive richness from their relationship with God. In conversation after conversation, I'm pleasantly surprised at the level of experiential diversity: where one person felt the richness of God through worship, another experienced it more through fellowship; while another felt it in prayer, others said it was in nature, and others in times of trial.

One common thread I did uncover during these transparent conversations is that people do have specific activities where they experience a heightened sense of God's presence, a place where his richness, guidance, and interaction are operating in an abundance that defies logic and brings both fruit and the fruit of the Spirit to the forefront. Those I surveyed experienced God in diverse ways, but there was one commonality in almost all of them: 90 percent of the people I asked said that God's presence, power, and peace became intensely alive when they were in the process of serving others. Results were scattered on experiencing a heightened sense of God's presence in worship, prayer, reading the Bible, nature, and so on, but it was in serving others where supernatural intervention was perpetual and uncommonly powerful. These people also made it clear that there was little chance of them bearing the kind of fruit they did in their serving without God's full intervention. It was here where lives were changed, miracles were seen, and an unbreakable confidence to serve in the fullness of their gifting was soaked in God's presence.

The outcome of giving is the gift we all share,
as to be born into a body of flesh only to someday
leave it means ultimately we may attain nothing
to keep in this life, except for what we give.
What we give lives on.

Another theme that showed up was in the form of a question. In some derivation, many would ask, "If this is where I experience God most, why don't I go there more, why don't I use my gifts more often?" God has made each of us brilliant in our gifts, and since you are part of the body of Christ, there are others who need you to go *there more often* with your gifts. Who are they? Where are they? The answer is simple: seek and you will find, pray and they will come, open your eyes and you will see, and you'll be impacting lives and experiencing God in profound ways, all through using the gifts, aptitudes, expertise, and intelligence you possess. *Use your gifting and see how God shows up today.*

The Question: Who and where are those in need of the gifts I have to give?

86. Creatively Loving Others

> When you carefully set up your life to bring value to yourself more than to others, you inadvertently remove the value right out of your life.

You, my brothers and sisters, were called to be free. But do not use your freedom to indulge the flesh; rather, serve one another humbly in love.

Galatians 5:13

If I look at my life closely at any given time, I will find various methods and strategies I am implementing to make sure I am getting what I need, but more realistically, much more than I need. I find myself seeking excess that not only doesn't satisfy my spirit, it ends up as a never-ending quest to satisfy self: a downhill spiral that leads to loneliness, discouragement, and eventually depression.

It's not flawed thinking to want to create a fulfilled life for ourselves, but upon further inspection we may notice that it can be a deterrent to the creative ways we can serve into the lives of those around us. This is where accommodating the needs of self and delivering value to others meet at the intersection of healthy relationships and sustainable fulfillment—where God says, "Well done," and good fruit is everywhere.

> You don't love others necessarily because they deserve it, you love others because you deserve it . . . and God commands it.

The intelligence of God never ceases to amaze me, especially the things he said that seem contradictory to our normal mode of thought but actually work. One straight-up example is the directive for us to count others as more important than ourselves. Hmmm! How does that work? More important? That doesn't seem to add up.

While at the gym one morning I asked a man if he found any value in the statement that we are to count others as more important than ourselves. He answered, "That's a ridiculous statement. What is that, a Bible verse? We live in a world where we need to look out for ourselves." I responded by asking a simple question: "So how does that work *for you*, that looking-out-for-yourself thing?" After a bit of conversation, I discovered he was recently divorced and estranged from two of his three children. I told him I was sorry to hear he was going through all that and chose to revisit the conversation at a later date. He was raw, bitter, defensive, and unable to hear much at the time . . . all while he was looking out for himself rather than considering the alternative. He had paid a big price and was still paying—as was his family.

Because God is creative, we are creative, and we've been given an innate ability to design and innovate the most creative and compelling ways to love, care for, and impact others. God, in his infinite wisdom, knew that the directive to *count others as more important than ourselves* would ultimately satisfy most of our needs in life, business, and relationships. And it will, as long as we bring it front of mind, get creative, deliver the value, and reap the harvest. It's all there for us, and for others. *Consider those around you as opportunities to serve today.*

The Question: Might my life be more fulfilling and exciting if I seized more opportunities to love and be a blessing to others?

87. Engaging the Holy Spirit

> Why do we open books but
> shut out the Holy Spirit?

But the Advocate, the Holy Spirit, whom the Father will send
in my name, will teach you all things and will remind you of
everything I have said to you.

John 14:26

It's no surprise that the quest for knowledge and life guidance is
enhanced by the vast number of options available. Although the
resources are nearly limitless, the dependability and quality of
information will always be uncertain and will generally require a
moderate dig before we know whether a resource will serve our
lives the way we expect it to. The investment of time we have
into this kind of learning begs the question, "What if I took the
time I invested in the next best seller, workshop, podcast, or other
learning resource and devoted that time to learning and practicing
engaging and communing with the Holy Spirit?"

Among the more underutilized opportunities we have in life is
slowing down enough to commune and dialogue with the Holy

Spirit. The good news: we don't have to download the Holy Spirit, go to the store, or make a purchase. In fact, he's located in the soul nearest you. He's always in, always open for business, and is the nth degree of wisdom, patiently waiting for us to acknowledge his presence and tap into an endless inventory of insights, comfort, and innovation. He's not a fad, a latest-and-greatest this or that. He is current, relevant, and has a pulse on our past, present, and future. He knows the inner workings of the world in real time, always. In the most pragmatic sense he is the beginning of our clarity, the end of our chaos, and the sustainer of our peace. And yet most Christians I talk to tell me they cannot connect the dots on connecting with the Holy Spirit. I can relate; I couldn't for most of my life.

All the power of God is available to us 24/7.

Many years ago, I met with a Christian CEO coach. After I told him my story and a sample of my day, he shared that his experience of me was that I proclaimed to be a spiritual man but had no real spiritual foundation and that I was going solo through life, suffering in my own strength, and accessing little (if any) of the power, resolve, and creativity God had for me. Needless to say, he was spot-on and had my attention, so I invited him to share more. He went on to tell me that I had built my entire system of strength and learning around what the world had to offer and was at the point in my life where God wanted more for me; with a pause he said powerfully, "And you want more for you." In short, he told me it was time to turn pro or things would get further rooted in futility. I agreed and told him breakfast was on me (as indicated by the egg on my face).

Before we parted, he challenged me to get in a room, clear my head of debris, become "unreasonably" still, and ask the Holy

Spirit this question: "What do you want me to know about X today?" The X could be whatever, but in this case it was my wife. To my surprise, God answered, not out loud, but in my thoughts. The feedback was brief, powerful, and divinely wise. This exercise began a new lifelong dialogue that tells me many things I need to know if I am willing to slow down enough to catch the current of God's flow. And in asking him how I should close this out, he simply wanted to tell you, *I'm always here.*

The Question: As I go about my life, am I outpacing the Holy Spirit, never allowing him the front position as my Counselor/Collaborator/Comforter?

88. Shifting Gears in Our Thought Life

*In*security.

> Finally, brothers and sisters, whatever is true, whatever is noble, whatever is right, whatever is pure, whatever is lovely, whatever is admirable—if anything is excellent or praiseworthy—think about such things.
>
> Philippians 4:8

Imagine a life where any insecurity that popped up could be managed into peace and total confidence in a minute or two. That might sound like imagining you're driving an Indy car at two hundred miles an hour with fifty other drivers in close quarters when you're accustomed to driving in mild traffic at sixty-five miles an hour max, sipping a latte. Adjusting to new perspectives that fast may sound impossible, but given a commitment to practice renewing our mind, we would be able to more effectively control the negative thoughts we create in our life, those that others bring into our life, or the ones that simply enter our life through circumstances. But none of the drivers of those Indy cars came to race at that level without diligent and repetitive practice. Renewing our mind is no different.

Not to assume you have any, but if you were to initiate the process of dealing with a current insecurity or two, you might start changing things around you: get a new job, change out relationships, eliminate problem spots or problem people, remove areas of uncertainty, and so on. All of these may perhaps be wise to do. But after you succeeded, you'd have a week or two of optimistic reprieve only to discover that after contending with those issues, insecure feelings are creeping back—and in some cases, they come back stronger than before. Removal doesn't always eradicate permanently.

That which you give your mind to will
consume you—good or bad!

The truth is, no amount of external change will bring lasting relief to insecurity, nor will rearranging what we perceive as liabilities. This has to be dealt with from the inside out, not the outside in. Much of the time, it's a spiritual matter of heart and mind. As for the seriousness of this work, when you hear the Scripture that tells us to take every thought captive, the word *captive* means to take an enemy to the ground, with a spear pointed directly at the jugular vein in the neck. This is the starting point and the degree of intention that is required for us to develop the spiritual habit of renewing our minds, which allows us to go from fear to confidence much sooner.

This should be reassuring, as shifting thoughts is easier, faster, and more predictable given we engage in the practice needed to be more proficient. Renewing our minds in accordance with God's Word and promise is a worthwhile work of the inside that will have exponential value for all things on the outside. It is the play on the old adage garbage in, garbage out, and whatever garbage inside is sabotaging the outside cannot just be removed, it must be replaced. "What new thinking is required for change?" *Give serious effort to renewing your mind and marvel at the speed of change.*

The Question: What amount of time do I spend replacing thoughts that don't serve me with the specific thoughts God has given me?

89. The Heart of War

> There's a warrior inside for the battle outside.

Sovereign Lord, my strong deliverer, you shield my head in the heart of battle.

Psalm 140:7

Have you ever woken up in the morning, cleared your eyes, and said, "Well, it's off to battle?" Neither have I, consciously. But subconsciously, I know I do it every day. However, I do believe we'd be wise to include that in our conscious daily preparation, as the most prevalent war ever fought in the history of humankind has been and will always be fought on the battleground of the mind. Instead, our often latent view of life can numb us to the reality that *we are at war*. Despite the intensity of such a thought, we can have a calm recognition of this war and how well equipped we are to fight, *and win*.

The effectiveness of the weapons of warfare is directly associated with our awareness and acknowledgment of our arsenal.

God calls us to armor up daily: the belt of truth, the breast-plate of righteousness, feet shod with peace, the shield of faith, the helmet of salvation, and the sword of the Spirit. Frankly, it doesn't sound like we're off to a baby shower now, does it? *But that would depend, I suppose, on the baby shower and perhaps who might be there.*

In contrast to biblical times when exposure to evil demonic forces was limited to human interaction, today's technology and mass communication deliver a steady stream in every blink of an eye. The volume of incoming threats against our peace, integrity, and witness as Christians is alarming, and the future will only bring more intensity—another promise of warfare we should not ignore. Although we are not stepping out into a physical battle-field, the mental and spiritual war we face is enough to take us out emotionally at any time. The world is a fallen one, and coming to grips with that truth should put us on high alert for how we've been equipped to deal in a fallen world, operating in God's promise that we truly have dominion over ALL the earth.

The wisdom of preparing for battle each day and amassing enough spiritual strength to withstand the day's attack is admi-rable. But to step out with enough fortitude to help others in their war is noble and where we need to be: always with a surplus of the fruit of the Spirit, a spiritual medic ready to dispense healing, encouragement, and strength to those in the war with us. This is the warrior of today's world. *This is you today!*

The Question: Do I wake up each day with the acknowledgment that I am going to war and will have victory, or is my approach so casual that I feel overwhelmed, unprepared to fight?

90. The Value of Obedience

Have you ever wondered what's on the other side of improvements in obedience?

If you love Me, keep My commandments.

John 14:15 NKJV

There have been times in my life when my disobedience ranked from mild to wild. Either way, I felt ungrounded, devoid of conviction, and unplugged from God and others. After I shared my sin for feedback and accountability, I found that the people who knew me sensed something was amiss prior to my sharing but couldn't put their finger on it. In other words, we can't hide it from others when repetitive sin is in our life. It instills a subtle awkwardness or an apparent despair into our spirit, and it creates a weakening in our effectiveness and presence that will not be fully removed until the sin stops. The problem here is that we rarely stop the sin long enough to see that the value of abstinence supersedes the value of the sin. All sin has value to us—otherwise we wouldn't do it.

The strange thing is that there are numerous references in the Word that support how God honors obedience. Then there are times in the Scripture when he blesses people who are smack-dab in the middle of sinning. Not to say that while sinning there may be blessings or an absence of consequences, but there seems to be no absolute formula here.

One thing I can say with complete certainty, though, is there has always been a consistent peace and resolve in my life when I choose not to engage in certain ongoing sins and choose to expose my breakdowns to trusted others for prayer, counsel, and course correction. Life seems to be simpler, relationships are more honest, my words have greater impact . . . *everything is better.* However God deals with us as individuals in the area of sin (and deal he will, one way or another, sooner or later), he does it because he loves us and wants the best for us.

Obedience opens pathways to see new insights, experience new blessings, and remove tired, old thinking.

Regardless of what versions of disobedience we toy with, I'm convinced that if we experienced what was on the other side of a commitment to release recurring sin into God's hands and moved to take new territory, we'd look back over the obedience fence and say, "No thanks to that old sin—I think I'll stay right here." And as we turn around and move to newer ground where another obedience fence reveals itself in the distance, we might say, "Well, being on this side of obedience was good; perhaps what's on the other side of that one will be good too." And it will be even better, as obedience has a way of compounding value for us and those around us. *Move to a new level of obedience today and see what shows up and what doesn't.*

The Question: Have I considered stopping that recurring belief or action for about ninety days to see what God does during that time and on the other side of it?

91. The Power of the Right Heart

With the right heart, nothing is impossible.

> Blessed are the pure in heart,
> for they will see God.
>
> Matthew 5:8

Some years ago, a friend of mine was invited to the first round of CEO interviews for a national ministry. When I heard he was a candidate for the job, I was uncertain about his capacity to fulfill the specific demands of the job. Granted, his character was solid, work ethic exemplary, but his history of work had little to do with being at the helm of a national entrepreneurial organization, let alone one with such an unconventional model. And yet he got the job. To say I was nervous for my friend was an understatement, yet he landed the position—one that could make a notable difference in the world—with high stakes and an even higher gradient of intensity.

Like most new CEOs, his first year was spent in due diligence— traveling the country, listening, and planning based on what he was learning. His diligence to listen to the heart of the entire

267

organization led to some very clear realizations about how things had been in the past. When he found out that the organization was growing but not yet on solid ground, financial stewardship was the first order of business, and things moved to stability in relatively short order. Another realization was that there was a relational disconnect between leadership and the national network of team members. Wanting a culture of intimacy, my friend implemented events, processes, and best practices that would ensure that the network had a voice and was able to share their concerns and desires to corporate, where things could be implemented, and most importantly, changed.

> Results vary when you put the cart before
> the horse but become extraordinary when
> you put the heart before the course.

Along with that, my friend's character had led to relationships over the past three decades that were leveraged into new channels of growth and development that were quite innovative for an organization of its kind. Staff changes were made, board positions were added, the office location was changed, and the mission, vision, and values were overhauled and aligned to the entire organization. All within two years.

When you have a heart and a commitment as exampled by my friend, three things happen simultaneously. First, the heart pushes through obstacles like a speeding train would through bales of hay. Second, those around you contagiously tap into the same heart and bring a loyalty and commitment to you that is virtually unstoppable. Third, God looks down on a humble and willing heart and supernaturally infuses tools, assets, connections, and resources into the mix because when we care for all things well, he adds much more to the equation. *Bring the heart you are putting behind all things to a new place today and see what God can do with your current capacity.*

The Question: Is there room to add more care, stewardship, and heart to the things I'm currently doing?

92. Reducing Chronic Fear

> Many people have phobias—I'm afraid it's true.

Humble yourselves, therefore, under God's mighty hand, that he may lift you up in due time. Cast all your anxiety on him because he cares for you.

1 Peter 5:6–7

A phobia is a subtle-to-severe fear with root causes that range from catastrophic experiences to no explanation whatsoever. They differ from circumstantial, occasional fears in that they are chronic, and in many cases they are completely unfounded. A simple Google search will give indication that about 10 percent of all people suffer from a phobia. I have a contrary belief based on my own experience as a counselor, but I believe that EVERYONE has phobias at some level and those who say they don't have any are simply *afraid* to share them. ☺ Regardless, phobias come in all shapes and sizes and manifest in varying degrees of intensity from subtle tones of discomfort to paralyzing, life-stopping forces. Public speaking, death, spiders, flying, using public restrooms, computers, drinking from glass containers, suffocating from carpet fibers, heights, caves—there are literally thousands, and the bizarre and diverse nature of them is vast. They are rarely talked about, concealed with great effort, and can hinder us for a lifetime without ever being brought into the light.

Despite whether we categorize the problem as psychological, emotional, or spiritual, there are natural *and* spiritual ways to contend with, even overcome phobias. Cracking the hardened structure of phobias begins by embracing them as a provision—trusting that God will use them for his purpose in your life and the lives of others. And he will, but we can sabotage his work by standing as a victim to our fears rather than believing what God has to say about them. It is in appreciation for these fears (as much of a curse as they may seem), that we remove the dreaded curse upon the curse. Now we get to deal with the phobia without the stress and self-condemnation, focusing on only the fact that we have it and it's not so bad. There's freedom in that alone.

Fear itself doesn't exist on the earth, only in
how we process the things on earth.

Next we should get vulnerable and share our phobias with *trusted* friends or *wise* or *professional* counselors. This will be unnerving at first, but with every conversation, the stronghold weakens, new perspectives are revealed, and the shame of sharing dissipates to near nothing. I know from my own experience and the experience of others that this is true. God does great work in honest conversations, and they are a stimulant for others to share more openly, moving relationships to a deeper, more meaningful level.

Studying the phobia and connecting with others who struggle with the same issue are other parts in loosening the stronghold, as are small incremental steps of exposure to the phobia. There are several things that can increase our faith, but one that can multiply it is found in the process of addressing our phobias head-on. While taking the natural steps of healing, we can engage in the spiritual steps of highly specific prayer, praise of victory in advance, and reading God's Word and other material that relates directly to the fear. Together, these things are a deadly combination for moving phobias into a manageable state or wiping them out altogether. It can be done. *Embrace your fears, see their value, be at ease with them, and set a plan to contend with just one of them today. If you have one of course.*

The Question: If I set out to move a phobia to a less-powerful force or eliminate it altogether, what would that plan look like for me?

93. Owning Your Stress Level

Ultimately, stress is a choice . . . as is joy.

You were taught, with regard to your former way of life, to put off your old self, which is being corrupted by its deceitful desires; to be made new in the attitude of your minds; and to put on the new self, created to be like God in true righteousness and holiness.

Ephesians 4:22–24

Combine the sinful nature of man, our general experiences in life, current world conditions, and of course our wonderfully optimistic media, and you'll begin to understand the need to combat stress and cynicism. By the time we hit early adulthood, the hard drive of our mind is so full of reasons not to be happy that caving to doubt and mental tension seems like an easier path than renewing our minds.

Negative thoughts don't mind entering
your mind if you don't mind.

FACT: Your mental hard drive is the lens you look at your world through and is the determinant of most every emotion and behavior. FACT: Old or newly formed data is not pushed off the hard drive until it is replaced with new data that has greater relevance and value than the old. FACT: Reprogramming your hard drive is an ongoing process for the believer. FACT: The incoming addition of new data never stops, but we choose what gets in. FACT: Adding biblical truth onto the hard drive accelerates the deletion of old destructive data. The only question is, how often are you adding to the hard drive? **FICTION**: God is responsible for your hard drive. **FICTION**: Others are responsible for your hard drive. **FICTION**: Your hard drive will change with a casual commitment. FACT: In a given day, there are literally hundreds of opportunities to reprogram your hard drive. FACT: It's reprogrammed one decision at a time.

We've touched on renewing our minds a few times, but I wanted to reopen the topic because the challenge never ends and I wanted to make certain it was clear that we are solely responsible for standing at the gates of our minds to control what enters and what doesn't. For example, if the word *media* stands for Manipulates Everyone Directly Into Anxiety (my own definition, of course), then it would make sense to find a delivery system for news that is fact based, not emotion based. The same goes for people we hang with, activities we're involved in, and the things we read, listen to, or watch: it's the small decisions of exposure that make a big difference. Want proof? Fast from media, negative people, and less-than-godly circumstances for a month and notice the condition of your mind and spirit. You'll see a reduction or removal of stress, confusion, and uncertainty, and your mind will have added bandwidth to devote to the more important things of life. *Consider fasting from the things that bring you stress this week, month, year, or life.*

The Question: Stress is what happens when a mind relaxes too far into a place of complacency. What would a proactive renewing of my mindset look like?

94. Avoiding the Traps of Ministry

Don't let your ministry turn into misery.

We have different gifts, according to the grace given to each of us.

Romans 12:6

We've covered the idea that ministry is found in the posture of our hearts to serve in all moments at all times. But there is *vocational ministry* guidance that can provide a greater degree of effectiveness over a longer period of time while experiencing a more rewarding, less taxing journey. It will require, however, that we give serious scrutiny to the process of getting into a vocational ministry and draw some hard lines if needed—meaning the value of thinking it through on the front end will prevent a miserable dead end.

The ministry leader/participant burnout rate today is alarming, as is the declining percentage of people who enter into vocational ministry, let alone the church. Reasons range from the simple to the complex, but the need for the Christian body to be functioning at full capacity, fulfilling a diversity of needs, has never been more apparent.

Every day, thousands of Christians enter into new ministries with an uncertainty of what their gifting is and where they might fit best in the long term. In fact, most get into a ministry position inside or outside the church as a means to "become involved," or with a more dangerous motive: as a way to define themselves. Many succumb to pressure from leaders who have little or no insight about whether the person has ample passion and gifting for certain positions. As a result, the person's enthusiasm often turns to burnout, their new relationships can turn to broken ones, and their identity takes another blow straight to the spirit—while their real ministry potential stays dormant until the wounds from the previous experience heal (and that can take a while).

> Any potential to last in ministry generally shows up
> as "Cool, I get to . . . ," versus "Darn, I have to . . ."

Deep contemplation, prayer, and feedback from others should be paramount when evaluating the ministry positions that are presented to us or that we are considering. We should understand the full details of the position, the expectations, and what the success measures might look like from those to whom we will report. We should get to know the players involved, carve out the time to ask questions of others in similar ministry positions, and do adequate due diligence into all aspects of the ministry so we have an absolute peace and release from God for the position. Knowledge is key here.

Ministry will always be more effective, enjoyable, and sustainable if it falls within our unique God-given gifting or the learned skills and abilities we have come to enjoy: those things we are good at that will help other people. God gave all of us gifts, and the church body needs those gifts—not just for a week or a season, but for a lifetime. *Do a proper evaluation of the ministry you're in or are considering being in today.*

The Question: Does the ministry I am in or am seeking lean more toward life-giving or life-draining for me?

95. Finding Value in the Midst of Problems

> Problem + Perspective − Pessimism = Provision

Consider it pure joy, my brothers and sisters, whenever you face trials of many kinds, because you know that the testing of your faith produces perseverance. Let perseverance finish its work so that you may be mature and complete, not lacking anything.

James 1:2–4

Problems manifest in limitless ways. Some of them are very real, while others, as mentioned earlier, are a complete fabrication of thought that can have equal or more intensity than a problem that's actually happening. Many are a blend of reality and problematic thinking. At least when things are real we can define them with some sense of limit to their impact. Mentally invented problems, on the other hand, feel limitless. Knowing that an imagined event can record itself in your mind as real should reveal to us that invented problems may have the greater effect on our lives. Mark Twain penned a wise perspective when he wrote, "I am an old man who has known many problems, most of which never happened." But there's an opportunity here: what we can invent or create one way, we can invent or create in a different way.

The only problem with problems is we see them as a problem and that's the problem.

During any difficult time (real or imagined), perhaps the most sensible question we can ask as Christians is this: If this trial, obstacle, or challenge were a learning lesson from God in some way, what would God be wanting me to learn? And how would God want to use this potentially painful yet precious experience to build a godlier me? Within every trial that comes our way, there is distinct value that blurs the problem and makes the blessings clear if we are open-minded, seeking what God desires to do for us amidst the issue. In fact, in every trial there is intrinsic value for our spiritual growth that cannot be acquired any other way. Reading, therapy, seminars, and the most recent learning trends cannot instill into your presence what a "well-played" trial can.

Unfortunately, much of the value of trials is missed because we lay victim to problems rather than look for God's provision *in them*. We consent to allow the pain, stress, and confusion of the trial to overshadow its value, blessing, and growth due to nothing more than a shortsightedness of God's perfect plan for our lives. Our vision becomes obscured because we choose to stare deep into the pain rather than look past it to see what we will be on the other side. There is always another side of a trial that is of value, even if that side happens to be heaven.

God wants you to derive irreplaceable value from the challenges of life, he wants to use you as part of the blessing process and as a testimony for others to see the power of God's hand, the resolve of our faith, and the beauty of what it means to *actually believe* in biblical perspectives relating to trials. *Treat a problem in your life as a provision today.*

The Question: What is my problem default mode? Do I move straight into what is wrong, how bad it is, and how long it will last? Or do I default into the reality that God is up to something here that will bless me?

96. The Value of Straight Talk

> Political correctness does not
> belong in the church.

Instead, speaking the truth in love, we will grow to become in every respect the mature body of him who is the head, that is, Christ.

Ephesians 4:15

When I envision Jesus communicating, I imagine him operating from a grounded place of love, where he could speak anything to anyone and the heart from which it was spoken ensured it would be received as intended. The heart, when exercised in its full potential, can create the space for most anything to be said effectively. We will always have an advantage of being able to say just about anything to anyone as long as we are in the right heart while in the process. Although I want to believe that courage is present in believers to speak truth, there is an epidemic in the church of not wanting to say things that desperately need to be said to others for fear of backlash, looking bad, conflict, and discomfort—all fears of self that have no place in the believer's life and hinder us from being effective in our discernments and in the body.

In the modern day, we've branded this practice *political correctness*. Defined more accurately, it is the practice of self-protection, cover-up, and masking our truth into statements of nothing, and it's making life and relationships beige, blurry, and bleak as well as ineffective. Not to say that basic social graces are out of vogue, they are vital, but to converse with someone who has packaged their words with "play it safe sanitation" does little compared to a bit of graceful forthrightness. To be in true communion with one another means truth and honesty are the foundation versus tentativeness and concealment, which serve nobody.

> A true friend is someone who tells you forthrightly what you won't admit to yourself.

In the long run, people would rather be with those who share their truth at the risk of being wrong or looking foolish instead of those who design their conversations around looking good, protecting self, appearing intelligent, and offending no one. "What you see is what you get" is a breath of fresh air that brings life to people and moves the church to deal in directness, not delusions. We need feedback from others, they need it from us, and we should be comfortable in the right heart posture to share what we see.

Mark my words, as each year of this complex new world passes, the popularity of political correctness is going to dip below dirt and the thirst and implicit need for "give it to me straight" communication is going to spike through the atmospheric shield. The courage to put your full truth on the table will be among the more valued assets on the planet. In fact, it already is, and we need to voice that. *Honesty needs to be shared in your life. Ground yourself in love and serve others by sharing it today.*

The Question: In what ways and with whom am I not sharing the fullness of my truth—walking on eggshells or perpetuating a false relationship?

97. Freedom in Sowing

> There's no business like sow business. (Sorry, it was there.)

Remember this: Whoever sows sparingly will also reap sparingly, and whoever sows generously will also reap generously.

2 Corinthians 9:6

When we think of sowing, we know that it's some form of delivering the love and the heart of God into the lives of others by way of our gifting or what God puts on our hearts to do or be. But then there's that reaping thing that seems a bit more abstract. Reap what, exactly? Eternal reward? Or might it be some other form of acknowledgment or expectation we might have? Should we even be concerned with what we reap, or simply sow and not know to avoid the disappointments that could show up if we were caught up in expectations of what we should receive?

Sowing into another's life should not be awkward ground, but it *can* be. We can be misunderstood, we can sow with poor execution, sow with the wrong heart, use the wrong approach at the wrong time, and more. But the biggest trap of sowing is the expectation that others will be the ones to show appreciation, reciprocate, or acknowledge our efforts. Add to that those creative inventions we make up about the ways we *should be acknowledged* for what we sow, and it may have others around us saying, "Keep your sowing to yourself."

> You're always making a difference with others. It's either a positive difference or a negative difference, but make no mistake about it, a difference is being made one way or the other.

Any Christian who's been consistently active in "Sow Biz" should know by now that sowing with any type of expectation from others is not just a saboteur of the potential fruit and blessings but the beginning of bitterness, resentment, and the looming disease of "If others don't start acknowledging what I do for them the way I think is appropriate, then I'm just going to stop giving." Tragically, many have ceased or placed conditions on serving because appreciation from others wasn't visible enough, fast enough, often enough, or public enough to fulfill their need to be valued. We all know that sowing into the lives of others can be a trap in which Christians make others a mechanism of their fulfillment, and yet there is little fulfillment found here.

Consider that in God's way of giving, we are to sow into others knowing full well others are just a conduit or means to sow straight into the kingdom of God. Now consider that God himself will determine when and how he is to acknowledge, affirm, and bless you for your actions and that his promise to do so will not be broken, despite what we make of that. Might there be more peace in trusting the Lord for our blessings than being distracted from life, impatiently waiting for the email, phone call, note, or conversation about how much impact you think you may have had? For all kinds of reasons, others will generally under-deliver, especially when they are set up to fail with our insatiable need to be affirmed.

It shows great insight when we know who acknowledges and compensates us for our sowing into the kingdom. I'm sure we would all sow more selflessly knowing our reward is birthed in eternity, not in humanity. There is a supernatural blessing on the way, and whatever you get from humankind is just the icing on the cake. *Sow well today.*

The Question: Can I release the blessing of my sowing into God's hands, or will I continue to be disappointed at the inconsistent levels of response I receive from others?

98. Accounting for Our Actions

> Taking ownership of what shows up in life, business, and relationships means never being a victim to the circumstances.

Do not be fooled. You cannot fool God. A man will get back whatever he plants!

Galatians 6:7 NLV

This point hits rather hard, and I wanted to state upfront that aside from those who are truly victims where things happened beyond their choice, control, or participation, we are responsible for everything that shows up in our life, good or bad, big or small. The fact that God gave us free will mandates that we accept his word as 100 percent true on the accountability part of sowing and reaping. Although this sounds elementary, and God's Word is clear, there are these things called excuses, justifications, exaggerations, rationalizations, conditions, and a bunch of other reasons people use to negate why certain results happen. The worst culprit is pinning poor results or bad things happening to us on God's will. This is not only untrue of God's nature, it's an escape of accountability that will bring a person's growth to a quick halt or slow crawl.

If you want to discover the true impact of your choices, look at what shows up in others as you engage with them and what shows up in your life as you make decisions.

In counseling and mentoring sessions, I've heard hundreds of stories about why marriages failed, businesses went south, children became estranged, relationships broke apart, and dreams died, and even why conversations didn't turn out so well. Rarely if ever does someone, after stating the problem, say to me, "Dean, I'd like to explore how it was that I sowed into the situation such that I reaped. I'd like to discover the ways I was responsible so I can stop doing this or do this differently so I will have different results." The few people who have said this are the people who turned out to be grounded, peaceful, and fulfilled, and who moved forward in life instead of being stuck or moving backward. On the flipside, those who blamed others or circumstances for their results were scattered, agitated, and growing at the speed of a dead turtle. Seems many humans loathe being wrong and want to place blame outside of themselves. There is no resolve, hope, or growth in that.

There will always be true revelation and progress when we account for how our actions, behaviors, and beliefs have impacted our life and relationships. Even if we caused or allowed a small percentage of the breakdown, if we admit our part, we will get in the habit of always refining our life and character instead of making excuses for it. Admitting our role in things also creates a safer space for others to be honest about their participation. It's the high road and the path to great possibilities when we own the results of our choices. *Take account for what shows up around you today.*

The Question: Am I looking first to myself for the results that are happening in my life or blaming God, others, and my past for what's going on?

99. The Pace of Life

> What's the rush, we live for eternity!

And this is what he promised us—eternal life.

1 John 2:25

I live in Orange County, California, and friends from out of state affectionately call it the rat race here. In many ways they're right; people and things move at a pretty accelerated pace, so much so that even the rats are exhausted.

But I don't think this "pace of life" issue is limited to Orange County. Anywhere you look, you'll find people who are moving at a rapid pace to get things done. More specifically, people want to get things "out of the way," because certain things seem "in the way" of a truly fulfilled life. And the tense way that we hold these things creates a barrier to the fruits of the spirit and distracts us from peace in our communion with God and others.

Some of the bigger things we want to happen in a hurry are for our finances to be secure, relationships to be healed, goals to be reached, positions to be attained, and status to be achieved. Then there's the smaller things like wanting to get our task list done for the day, the bills paid, the meal made, the phone call over with, etc.

> More often, the fastest way to get things done is to slow our minds to a place of calm, clear, innovative thinking. It's in this place where we discover the greatest efficiencies to get things done.

But it's never the actual activities that are the challenge, as they are static, nonemotional things. The challenge is the pace, stress, and tension we can attach to getting these things done that often derail our life and make us live as if there's never enough time. Crazy to think there's never enough time when we live for eternity.

Living eternally minded is a simple thing to do. Not easy, but simple. Living in eternity is not someplace we get to only when we stop breathing. When we acknowledge the truth that *living in a hurry* makes little to no sense, moving at a peaceful pace becomes a more rewarding and productive place from which to operate. It opens more mental and even physical capacity and energy to deal with all of life. It will help you find fulfillment in all things, embracing the journey of eternity, not rushing through it.

We have to remember when we are called to run the race to win, we should acknowledge that the race is not a series of mad dashes and tension-filled sprints, but more a marathon—a journey where our focus is less on the clock and the calendar, and more on eternity. *Live eternally minded today.*

The Question: Is moving at a frenetic speed really getting things done more quickly? Even if I think it is, is it worth the stress and pressure associated with the pace?

Final Thought

Since you're on this page of the book, I'm hoping this book has impacted your life in notable ways. That has been my commitment and my prayer for every reader. I'm also sure that along the way, you've read some of these points and thought they might impact others you know; perhaps you've even sent a few.

While writing this book, I thought of several people who I thought might be impacted by one of these points. Knowing the forthright nature of what I had written, I felt it important to be sensitive, read what was written in light of that specific person, and perhaps tee up what I was sending with a few words or a paragraph sharing the thinking behind what I was sending. I'd encourage you to prayerfully consider doing the same if you decide to share, as a little sensitivity and clarification can go a long way in making that difference.

Another way you can share what you've read is to give away your copy, send a link to the book, or purchase it for others. Regardless of the way you choose, of all the differences that we can make in someone's life, the best one is generally . . . *the next one.*

With growth in mind,
Dean Del Sesto

A Few Words on My Background

My brother Dave, the CPA, got the left-brain gene in the family. As for me, I'm a right-brain, creative thinker; I lean more lunar than linear, more pictures than spreadsheets, less logical and more philosophical. I started in business as a graphic designer, then turned writer, turned creative director, turned large-agency cofounder and CEO—meaning I picked up a few of those "left-brain" skills along the way.

I find few things more rewarding than helping people get from Point Anywhere, to Point Better in life, business, and relationships. With a personal mission statement that reads "To be a graceful interruption to whatever's not working in someone's business or personal life," I'm not the lightest guy in the room, but I'm committed to stopping the trajectory of anyone headed for difficulty and helping turn them toward the path of least resistance and most value in whatever they deem important.

Today, I run an award-winning brand- and business-development agency (venthio.com) that does all things branding and assists with marketing and revenue-generation strategy or implementation for medium to large companies. I am also a partner in a live-action and motion graphics video agency (veracitycolab.com) that does breakthrough video work for clients around the world.

My journey as an author started with my QuickShift emails sent to a moderately sized audience of clients, vendors, and anyone else who would read them. While talking with an author friend who'd been reading my emails and wanted to try his hand as a literary agent, I agreed to be his first client. Long story short, we submitted a book proposal for *Shift Your Thinking*, and eighteen months later, I was an author. Like any good agent, Joey told me, "Anyone can be a one-time author—everyone has *one* book in them—but are you a writer?" Thus, *Shift Your Thinking, Shift Your Thinking for Success, A Shift a Day for Your Best Year Yet,* and *Shift Your Thinking for a Deeper Faith* are all available.

I speak to both small groups and large audiences. If you think my brand of thinking might resonate with those you know, feel free to reach out via deandelsesto.com or venthio.com. My ministry talks are for audiences of any size and focus on the brand of Christianity, building a better marriage, various men's group topics, and other areas you have read about in this book, with lengths of thirty to ninety minutes. On the corporate side of my life, my talks focus on personal branding and business branding. I will speak from twenty to ninety minutes for audiences of any size, or hold smaller group sessions that last from one to three and a half hours at companies and organizations.

That's it for now. I wish you the best on your quest for better, and thank you again for reading *Shift Your Thinking for a Deeper Faith*.

DEAN DEL SESTO ™

SHIFT INTO OVERTHRIVE ™

"After creating over 800 brands, I've come to learn it's 'STAND OUT OR BE COUNTED OUT.' Every move, action, strategy, tactic, and detail will position you to be either selected or rejected depending on the resonance and relevance of your brand." —dds

---

To have Dean speak at your next event, visit

DEANDELSESTO.COM

Current topics include:

Building the Brilliant Brand of You for Breakthrough Business Performance

Focuses on tuning relational dynamics and interaction, character traits, brand persona, and effectiveness in business. Also shares ways of being that add value to career and relationships for greater effectiveness, fulfillment, and leverage.

Branding Your Business to Win More Business and Keep That Business

Speaks to brand realities, including identity, strategy, execution, building market and mind-share, and clarifies specifically how brand affects a company's bottom line. Also covers the importance of differentiation versus relevancy and why consistency is so vital to success.

YOU'RE JUST A
SMALL SHIFT AWAY
FROM SUCCESS

SMALL CHANGES,
BIG IMPACT

We all want to grow, improve, and succeed, yet so often the things we tell ourselves seem to stop our dreams in their tracks. But that can change. These two hundred to-the-point readings will help you shift your thoughts and behaviors so you can change the course of your life, work, and relationships—for good.

Learn more at **DEANDELSESTO.COM**